FIRST CORINTHIANS

FIRST CORINTHIANS

by

G. COLEMAN LUCK

MOODY PRESS

CHICAGO

ISBN: 0-8024-2046-X

Moody Press, a ministry of the Moody Bible Institute, is
designed for education, evangelization and edification.
If we may assist you in knowing more about Christ and
the Christian life, please write us without obligation to:
Moody Press, c/o MLM, Chicago, Illinois 60610.

Twelfth Printing, 1982

Printed in the United States of America

CONTENTS

Chapter One

INTRODUCTION

FIRST-CENTURY CORINTH was an important commercial center, with a population of 6- or 700,000. Typically Grecian in character, it was famed as a sport center, a fact which makes the allusion in I Corinthians 9:24-27 more pointed. Morals were deplorably low—the very name of the city became a synonym for luxurious dissipation. On the summit of Acro-Corinth stood the temple of Aphrodite, the goddess of beauty, where a thousand women prostitutes served as priestesses. The profligacy of the city furnished a great temptation to the early Christians there to be far too lax in their own morals.

The apostle Paul visited Corinth during the course of his second missionary journey. At that place he first made the acquaintance of a godly Christian couple, Aquila and Priscilla (Acts 18:2, 3), whose names are often used in his epistles. They evidently were already believers, as it seems certain that Luke would have mentioned the fact had Paul led them to the Lord. Aquila had been born at Pontus (the province northeast of Galatia). He later lived in Italy but had been forced to leave because of a decree by the Emperor Claudius. Suetonius, a Roman historian who wrote about A.D. 100, states that this decree was made because "the Jews (in Rome) were constantly in tumult at the instigation of one Chrestus," evidently a reference to *Christos,* or *Christ.* While in Corinth, Paul supported himself by working with Priscilla and Aquila at tentmaking, their mutual trade (notice allusions to this work in I Cor. 9:14, 15; II Cor. 12:13).

After his witness in the synagogue was rejected, he turned to the Gentiles, teaching at the home of a godly man, next door to the Jewish meeting place (Acts 18:4-7). This labor was richly rewarded: many were saved including even the ruler of the synagogue himself, along with his family (Acts 18:8). When Paul, however, became rather depressed and discouraged, he was granted an encouraging vision of the Lord, who assured him that "much people" would yet come to Christ through his testimony (Acts 18:9-11). This strengthened Paul to remain another year and a half at Corinth.

Finally however the Jews rose up against Paul, dragging him before the Roman proconsul, Gallio (Acts 18:12-18). Because of Luke's statement that "Gallio cared for none of those things," the latter has earned the appellation of "the careless Gallio." Far from being careless, Gallio was actually too clever to be deceived by the charges of the Jews. He immediately discerned that their accusations against Paul had to do with their own peculiar laws and customs rather than the Roman law, so he refused to hear their case at all.

Sosthenes succeeded Crispus after the latter's conversion as ruler of the synagogue. The mob turned on Sosthenes and gave him a beating. If he is the same man mentioned in I Corinthians 1:1, it seems that the whipping proved of value to him, for he later became a Christian himself. After that, Paul remained at Corinth "yet a good while," at last departing by boat for Syria, accompanied by his friends, Aquila and Priscilla.

During Paul's third missionary journey, about A.D. 57, he wrote from Ephesus his first epistle to the Corinthian church. Eventually he was permitted to visit Corinth again in person (Acts 20:1, 2). It is evident that he penned the epistle because of several important reasons. The most obvious purpose was to answer questions the Corinthians had addressed to him concerning problems in their church (7:1; cf. 8:1; 12:1; 16:1). These problems, in one form or another, are still more or less common to all churches today. His first objective, however, was to reprove a spirit of contentious factionalism, unhappily present at Corinth as a result of following human teachers in too partisan a manner (I Cor. 1:11-13). It was also urgent that he defend his apostleship and ministry, so unjustly attacked by false, legalistic teachers—the "judaizers."

The theme of this important epistle is *errors of Christian conduct corrected.* Paul rebukes such errors by showing that "God is not the author of confusion, but of peace, as in all churches of the saints" (I Cor. 14:33). Explicit instructions are given the believers as to how they may "let all things be done decently and in order" (I Cor. 14:40). The first four Pauline epistles in the New Testament have a close logical relationship. The first eleven chapters of Romans teach in a positive way the truth of *justification by faith;* the last five chapters outline the true course of *Christian conduct* and *service.* Galatians provides the necessary correction of *doctrinal error* concerning justification by faith; I Corinthians provides the correction for erroneous Christian *conduct;* II Corinthians, for Christian *service.* To put it in a slightly different way, I Corinthians teaches the proper "*order* in the church"; II Corinthians, the true "*ministry* in the church."

After a brief preface (1:1-9), seven forms of error are corrected. Paul in turn deals with errors concerning divisions (1:10–4:16); immorality (4:17–6:20); marriage (7); Christian liberty (8-11); spiritual gifts (12-14); the Gospel (15); and money (16:1-9). Certain closing admonitions (16:10-24) complete the epistle.

Chapter Two

PREFACE
(1:1-9)

A. Salutation (1:1-3)

PAUL, CALLED TO BE AN APOSTLE of Jesus Christ through
the will of God, and Sosthenes our brother, unto the
church of God which is at Corinth, to them that are sanctified in Christ Jesus, called to be saints, with all that in
every place call upon the name of Jesus Christ our Lord,
both theirs and ours: grace be unto you, and peace, from
God our Father, and from the Lord Jesus Christ."

In his letter to this church, Paul begins by voicing his
authority—he is a "called apostle." Since his apostleship
and ministry had been under fire, and it is now necessary
for him to exert that authority in correcting the serious
errors existing at Corinth, he commences by affirming that
he *is* truly an apostle, and that by no self-seeking of his
own, but "through the will of God." Sosthenes, a companion and fellow-worker of Paul, joins in the greeting
sent to this church. Obviously however he is not a *co-
author,* for Paul continually speaks in the first person
singular throughout the letter. As previously mentioned,
it has been conjectured that this Sosthenes is the same as
the Jewish leader of that name referred to in Acts 18:17,

who later became a convert and companion of Paul. This may well be true but cannot be finally proved.

The apostle writes to the "church *of God* which is at Corinth." It is not the church of any human leader or faction, but *of God.* The Greek word for *church* means "a called out assembly." Throughout this present age God is visiting "the Gentiles, to take out of them a people for his name" (Acts 15:14). This *church* is composed of "them that are sanctified." The word *sanctified* comes from the same root as *saint;* the key thought is that of *separation.* In its present usage it refers to the *position* of all true Christians—*separated—set apart* for holy service to God and holy fellowship with God. In other words, those who are *sanctified* are "called saints" (the words *to be* are in italics in the Authorized Version and should be omitted; this method is used to indicate words not in the original text of Scripture, but added to complete, as the translators thought, the English sense). The New Testament speaks of every true believer in Christ as a *saint.* In I Corinthians this is especially striking, as the reader soon learns that many of the members of that church were not *living* at all like *saints.* We *become* saints by believing on Christ as Saviour; once we *are* saints, then we should *live* like saints.

It is evident that the apostle intended that this letter should circulate beyond Corinth, as he includes in his greetings "all that in every place call upon the name of Jesus Christ our Lord." This includes every reader who is a true Christian. The expression "both theirs and ours" belongs with the word *Lord.* In a subtle rebuke of sectarianism, we are reminded that Christ is the *Lord* not just of some particular group or clique, but of *all* who believe on Him.

The apostle's greeting of *grace* was commonly used in that day by Greek people; *peace* was the salutation used by the Jews. Paul beautifully combines both words, giving them a much fuller meaning than they could possibly have carried in ordinary speech among non-Christian people. If *unsaved* we need grace and peace; even after we are saved, we still need them though in a somewhat different sense. It is interesting that the Bible always uses the terms in this particular order—grace must always come before peace, but grace when received is always accompanied by peace. The source of both is *God*—Father and Son.

B. Thanksgiving (1:4-9)

"I thank my God always on your behalf, for the grace of God which is given you by Jesus Christ; that in everything ye are enriched by him, in all utterance, and in all knowledge; even as the testimony of Christ was confirmed in you: so that ye come behind in no gift; waiting for the coming of our Lord Jesus Christ: who shall also confirm you unto the end, that ye may be blameless in the day of our Lord Jesus Christ. God is faithful, by whom ye were called unto the fellowship of his Son Jesus Christ our Lord."

In accordance with his usual custom, Paul opens his letter by commending the good things in the church. Afterward he will rebuke for objectionable features. But as always, he commends in such a way as not to glorify man but the Lord—he gives thanks to God, the real source of all blessing. He is thankful (*a*) for the grace of God given these people (and all other believers) by Jesus Christ, through whom alone God's grace comes to man.

This grace is evidenced by the fact that the Corinthians are "enriched by him." They are wealthy, not in worldly things, but "in all utterance"—they have a precious jewel of a message: the *Gospel*. They are rich too "in all knowledge." They know and understand the Gospel message and its implications. It is a great thing to know the Gospel, to grasp its meaning, to be able to proclaim it to other needy sinners.

Paul is thankful also that (b) "the testimony of Christ was confirmed in you," the result being that they "come behind in no gift." The expression "the testimony of Christ" means in the original construction "the testimony *concerning* Christ," a fact not perfectly clear in the English translation. The *power* of the "good news" about Christ was amply demonstrated in the Corinthian Christians— they were saved and abundantly gifted. All the various spiritual gifts were well represented in this church, as later chapters will make clear.

Paul is thankful that (c) the ones to whom he is writing are expectantly waiting for the Lord's coming. God is working in all true Christians to confirm, or guarantee, that we will all at that time be "blameless" (or "unreprovable") when we stand before Christ. The Lord Jesus has borne the *penalty* of our sins; our *failures* will be dealt with at the *judgment seat of Christ* so that in the end we will be *unreprovable*. Though men may fail we can count on this promise for "God is faithful." We have a glorious future! Even now our position is wonderful—we are called by God "unto the fellowship of his Son Jesus Christ our Lord."

Chapter Three

ERRORS CORRECTED: DIVISIONS
(1:10—4:16)

A. Existence of Divisions (1:10-17)

NOW I BESEECH YOU, BRETHREN, by the name of our Lord Jesus Christ, that ye all speak the same thing, and that there be no divisions among you; but that ye be perfectly joined together in the same mind and in the same judgment. For it hath been declared unto me of you, my brethren, by them which are of the house of Chloe, that there are contentions among you. Now this I say, that every one of you saith, I am of Paul; and I of Apollos; and I of Cephas; and I of Christ. Is Christ divided? was Paul crucified for you? or were ye baptized in the name of Paul? I thank God that I baptized none of you, but Crispus and Gaius; lest any should say that I had baptized in mine own name. And I baptized also the household of Stephanas: besides, I know not whether I baptized any other. For Christ sent me not to baptize, but to preach the gospel: not with wisdom of words, lest the cross of Christ should be made of none effect."

With a strong yet touching appeal for unity, Paul launches into the main body of his epistle. He lovingly urges all true believers in Christ, "brethren" in the Lord, to "speak the same things," and pleads that there be no "divisions" (or "splits") among them. This does *not* of course mean that every Christian must or will agree with every other believer on even the minutest point. It *does* mean that those who agree on the essential doctrines of the Christian faith should give a united testimony to the unbelieving world, not struggling and quarreling among themselves. Instead of an unhappy situation like that, the apostle urges true Christians to be "perfectly joined together." The expression suggests a jigsaw puzzle, with each piece different from the others and yet fitting and serving in its proper place to make a harmonious whole. "In the same mind" refers to the general *attitude* which should be one of humility (see Phil. 2:5-8). "In the same judgment" has reference to opinion or *understanding*. The Greek word here used is closely related to that for *knowledge*. True Christians should seek through God's Word to come to the knowledge of His will, and thus to mutual understanding with one another.

The reason for Paul's appeal in verse 10 becomes clear when verse 11 is read: "there are contentions among you." The original word does not mean simply differences of opinion but speaks of open *quarrels* or *wrangling*. To such a state their disagreements had brought them. The source of the apostle's information is said to be "the household of Chloe," but just which members of this household he had in mind, or even whether they lived in Corinth or Ephesus, is a matter of conjecture.

The Christians at Corinth were grouping themselves around various human leaders, and at the same time were rejecting other leaders and their followers. Directly mentioned in this regard are the names of *Paul, Apollos, Cephas,* and of *Christ* Himself. The basic message of each of these was certainly precisely the same, so the exact method the Corinthians used in distinguishing them is unknown. However it can reasonably be conjectured that those who were strong for the message of grace and justification by faith counted themselves followers of *Paul.* *Apollos,* an eloquent orator and native of Alexandria, ministered in Corinth after Paul had founded the church there (Acts 18:24—19:1). His adherents were perhaps the "intellectuals" who admired his marvelous speaking ability and his thorough knowledge of Greek philosophy. The humbler, uneducated Christians may likely have scorned the learned Paul and Apollos, preferring rough and ready *Peter,* considered by many to be the chief of the apostles. It may be also that those from Judaistic backgrounds preferred Peter to Paul because he seemed somewhat more favorable to Jewish forms and ceremonies (Gal. 2:11-14). Still others evidently said: "We reject all human teachers and leaders. We follow *Christ alone.*" They probably prided themselves on looking to the teachings of Jesus alone—or at least to *their* interpretation of His words.

All of these schools of thought find their counterpart in the modern church. Let us be reminded that we are to take no human teacher as our final, sole authority. All true teachers of God's Word are provided for the benefit of *all* (3:21, 22). And no one is to reject those who are true ministers of the Lord, piously pretending to follow Christ alone.

With three simple questions, Paul shows the absurdity of believers dividing over such matters. He asks: "Is Christ divided?" These Christians are behaving as if Christ is divided into different parts. This is utterly untrue—there is but one Body of Christ, composed of each one who truly believes on Him. "Was Paul crucified for you?" Human teachers, consecrated and effective as they may be, must decidedly take second place to Christ the supreme One, whose atoning death for our sins forms the very heart of the Gospel. If this is true, then should not all those cleansed by the precious blood of the Lord Jesus work together in harmony without fighting and quarreling? "Were ye baptized in the name of Paul?" The human minister who baptizes is of little importance compared with the One in whose name we are baptized.

But was it through some failure in the ministry of Paul that such difficulties had arisen in Corinth? Clearly not. He had been very careful, even in administering the sacrament of baptism, to do nothing that might seem an attempt to glorify his own human ministry, and thus to draw followers after *himself*. His one supreme work was to call men to Christ—to preach the Gospel. The sacraments themselves, important as they may be in their proper place, must remain secondary to this. The preacher must be careful even as he gives out the true doctrine of Christ lest he obscure it with "wisdom of words" and thus make the life-giving message ineffective. It is possible to proclaim the very truths of the Gospel in such a way that the eloquence and learning of the preacher become the predominant feature, and people are led to follow him rather than Christ.

B. Man's Wisdom Versus God's Wisdom (1:18-25)

"For it is written, I will destroy the wisdom of the wise, and will bring to nothing the understanding of the prudent. Where is the wise? where is the scribe? where is the disputer of this world? hath not God made foolish the wisdom of this world? For after that in the wisdom of God the world by wisdom knew not God, it pleased God by the foolishness of preaching to save them that believe. For the Jews require a sign, and the Greeks seek after wisdom: but we preach Christ crucified, unto the Jews a stumbling block, and unto the Greeks foolishness; but unto them which are called, both Jews and Greeks, Christ the power of God, and the wisdom of God. Because the foolishness of God is wiser than men; and the weakness of God is stronger than men."

That the divisions at Corinth were not the result of any dissension between the teachers the people professed to follow, Paul well knew. The true cause of the condition was that the believers were still engrossed with human, earthly wisdom. Now he undertakes to explain to them how futile and empty is such worldly wisdom.

In the phrase "the preaching of the cross," (v. 18) the word translated *preaching* is *logos* which means "word" or "message." The reference is then "not [to] the act of preaching, but the substance of the testimony, all that God has made known concerning the subject" (Vine's *Expository Dictionary of New Testament Words*). The apostle has already spoken of the *Gospel,* which centers around the *cross of Christ* (v. 17), around *Christ crucified* (v. 13). So then the "word of the cross" is the *message* of the *Gospel.*

To many people, this message of salvation through the death of Jesus Christ is "foolishness." This English word translates the Greek *moron* (from which we get by transliteration a familiar term). The word in the original language means *dull* or *stupid,* not foolish in the sense of comical. Paul does not mean that *because* these people are perishing, they consider the Gospel stupid, but rather that because they are worldly wise and reject the Gospel, *therefore* they are perishing. But those who are being saved, on the contrary, find the Gospel to be not foolishness, but the very power (Greek, *dunamis*) of God (cf. Rom. 1:16).

To make clear the futility of worldly wisdom, the apostle quotes Isaiah 29:14, slightly altering the original statement to make even stronger the truth it expresses: God will destroy and bring to nothing the mere worldly wisdom and prudence of unregenerate men. Rather satirically the apostle asks: "Where is the wise?" What has worldly wisdom and human philosophy accomplished—has it ever succeeded in really making the human race better or nobler? The *scribe* was the Jewish man of wisdom, the supposed authority on the law of God. Instead of helping men, he hindered them (Luke 11:45-54). The *disputer* is a reference to the Greek disputer or *sophist*, a clever philosopher. Was he truly able to help men? That he could not is demonstrated graphically by the fact that the very word *sophist* (lit., wise man) has come to mean "a captious or fallacious reasoner" (*Webster's Dictionary*). As we examine the vaunted "wisdom" of these renowned earthly wise men, can we not see that truly their wisdom is actually foolishness—stupidity—that God has made it so?

Thus God, in His heavenly wisdom, allowed the learned men of this world to seek by their worldly wisdom the solution to man's misery and suffering. But never were they able to discover the secret they sought—the end of all their teaching left man without a knowledge of the one true God who alone could give him life (John 17:3). Then God stepped in and by what worldly philosophers consider foolishness He proceeded to save and bless sinful people who were willing to believe on His Son, Jesus

Christ. As mentioned before, the word *preaching* as used here ("the foolishness of preaching") does not mean the act of proclaiming itself, but rather the message proclaimed—"the substance of what is preached, as distinct from the act of preaching" (Vine).

Both in Paul's day and at present, people are hindered from receiving this salvation by prejudice and by preconception. The *Jews* were perpetually looking for some material sign. They often asked Jesus Christ for such a sign, yet they were spiritually blind and refused to see the many signs He gave. The *Greeks* earnestly sought after wisdom—intriguing dialectics or cleverly involved reasoning—that would appeal to the intellect. The Gospel message of Christ crucified does not appeal to such people. The Jew finds it a *stumbling block,* that the *Messiah* should suffer and die on the cross of a common criminal. The Greek considers the message too simple, insufficiently intellectual, dull and stupid, in other words—*foolishness.* But then and now, thank God, there are many, both Jews and Gentiles, who will turn from these preconceptions to heed the message of salvation. Such find in Christ the very power and wisdom of God.

Paul's meaning in verse 25 is what worldly wise men consider the foolishness of God. It is in reality far wiser than the best thought that man unaided could ever produce. This answers the problem of the Greek. As for the Jew who cannot understand a Messiah so weak that He would allow Himself to be crucified by His enemies, Paul tells him that what may superficially appear to be weakness on the part of the Lord is actually a far greater exhibition of strength than the greatest thing man could ever do.

C. God Sets Aside Man's Wisdom (1:26-31)

"For ye see your calling, brethren, how that not many wise men after the flesh, not many mighty, not many noble, are called: but God hath chosen the foolish things of the world to confound the wise; and God hath chosen the weak things of the world to confound the things which are mighty; and the base things of the world, and things which are despised, hath God chosen, yea, and things which are not, to bring to nought things that are: that no flesh should glory in his presence. But of him are ye in Christ Jesus, who of God is made unto us wisdom, and righteousness, and sanctification, and redemption: that, according as it is written, He that glorieth, let him glory in the Lord."

These words really summarize the teaching the apostle is giving in this general section of the epistle. In verse 2 he spoke of the Corinthians as "called saints." Now he tells them "ye see your calling" or "behold your calling" (A.S.V.). By this he means "look at yourself, the ones whom God has called and blessed." There are among them "not many" whom the world considers wise or mighty or noble. In this sense Corinth was typical of the church as a whole throughout this entire age. The apostles themselves were considered by the Sanhedrin to be "unlearned and ignorant men" (Acts 4:13). In the Corinthian church there were "not many mighty"—the word refers to those who possess great power or influence. Also there were "not many noble"—that is, high born. Let us carefully observe that Paul did not say—"not *any*," but "not *many*." Lady Huntington, a wealthy and high-born friend of the Wesleys, used to say that she was saved by an *m*, for if this verse had not placed that letter before the *any*, she would never have been redeemed.

Generally speaking God has chosen as His servants those whom the world would call "foolish" or "base" (*base* here does not mean *evil* but rather of low or humble birth in contrast to *noble*). The Lord has however used these "foolish" and "base" ones to confound the mighty of the earth, even as Peter and John confounded the Sanhedrin. God is indeed even able to take "things which are not"—people whom the world considers so insignificant as to be beneath notice, "nobodies"—and to work in such a manner in their lives as to produce heroes of faith, who by deed and by word put to shame the proud and mighty of the earth.

The reason God does this is that "no flesh should glory in his presence." Justification is entirely by faith; furthermore the "just shall *live* by faith." If the Lord used very many who were mighty, wise, and noble, they might begin to think that it was by their own wisdom and power the work was being accomplished. By using "nobodies" God shows that the wisdom and power are entirely His own. Thus all the glory is His.

This then is the God with whom we have to do—"of him are ye in Christ Jesus." In the Lord Jesus we have the *true* wisdom, and *all* the wisdom we need. Of God "he is made unto us wisdom." This wisdom of God consists of "both righteousness and sanctification, and redemption." Through Him the believer is truly righteous, sanctified, and redeemed from sin. Human philosophy can never bring this to man. Therefore the Christian who boasts should never boast of himself but rather glory in the Lord; (Paul's statement here is a somewhat condensed quotation of Jer. 9:23, 24). In view of the futility of man's wisdom, and of the fact that we are nothing in ourselves but rather find in the Lord Jesus all we need, how unwarranted and uncalled for are contentions and divisions among true Christians! Thus always, in this section, is the apostle, either directly or indirectly, dealing with the problem of divisions in the Corinthian church.

D. The Central Theme of God's Wisdom and of Paul's Preaching (2:1-5)

"And I, brethren, when I came to you, came not with excellency of speech or of wisdom, declaring unto you the testimony of God. For I determined not to know anything among you, save Jesus Christ, and him crucified. And I was with you in weakness, and in fear, and in much trembling. And my speech and my preaching was not with enticing words of man's wisdom, but in demonstration of the Spirit and of power: that your faith should not stand in the wisdom of men, but in the power of God."

The "and I" with which this paragraph begins draws Paul himself to the reader's attention as a clear illustration of God choosing weak things. He again insists that the divisions in the Corinthian church did not come about because he ever encouraged such a spirit in his own personal ministry there. Never did Paul try to gather followers around himself. Having previously affirmed that he was careful not to give anyone ground to think he had "baptized in my own name" (1:15), he now explains that when he came to Corinth he did not try to use eloquent language so as to tickle the intellectual fancy of his hearers. Of a certain modern preacher it was said that "he had sacrificed the prophet to the artist." The apostle Paul disdained to use a lofty eloquence that while possibly winning him the praise of the intelligentsia would nevertheless have obscured the simple Gospel. He did not approach the Corinthians with philosophy, human wisdom, and learning, when he gave them "the testimony of God." Instead he deliberately determined "not to know anything save Jesus Christ, and him crucified." Of course, Paul is not saying here that certain fields of human knowledge are not useful in their proper place, neither is he belittling the value of other Christian doctrines besides that of the atonement. He himself preached "the whole counsel of God" (Acts 20:27, A.S.V.). He rather means that he determined always to *center* his preaching around the most important theme of all—the Person and atoning work of Jesus Christ. This was *foolishness* to the Greeks (1:23), so not only Paul's manner of speaking but his message itself was utterly contrary to the human wisdom the Corinthians so much admired.

After speaking of the message itself and of the language he used in presenting it (vv. 1, 2), Paul turns to his delivery showing that it likewise was not that of a professional orator, but of a weak instrument. By "weakness" (v. 3) he perhaps refers to some physical weakness connected with his "thorn in the flesh." The Greek word here translated *fear* is exactly the same as that used in the expression "be not afraid" in Acts 18:9, 10, which has to do with the apostle's stay at Corinth. "Trembling" could be taken in a literal sense but more likely should be understood figuratively as in II Corinthians 7:15. This frank confession of the apostle should serve us both by way of encouragement and of rebuke. When we consider on one hand the supreme importance of the message, and on the other our own weakness and limitations, we ought always to be in an attitude of utter dependence on God.

Paul's reference to his "speech" (v. 4) doubtless concerns his witness to individuals—what we usually call "personal work," while his "preaching" has to do with messages given to groups. While Paul deeply desired that his sermons might persuade men to receive Christ, yet he did not want to use "enticing" words—clever expressions such as a skillful orator might use to convince men of something that in actuality was unsound. He rather wanted to win men through the persuasive power of the Holy Spirit, as He dealt with the hearts of the hearers.

Furthermore Paul did not want his converts to place their faith "in the wisdom of men." Human wisdom changes from year to year. That which one season is considered scientific may be discredited the next. Any faith based on such "wisdom" would indeed have an extremely shaky foundation. "But in the power of God" is truly "the only secure place for faith to find a rest" (A. T. Robertson).

E. God's Wisdom Revealed to Us by the Holy Spirit (2:6-13)

"Howbeit we speak wisdom among them that are perfect: yet not the wisdom of this world, nor of the princes of this world, that come to nought: but we speak the wisdom of God in a mystery, even the hidden wisdom, which God ordained before the world unto our glory: which none of the princes of this world knew: for had they known it, they would not have crucified the Lord of glory. But as it is written, Eye hath not seen, nor ear heard, neither have entered into the heart of man, the things which God hath prepared for them that love him. But God hath revealed them unto us by his Spirit: for the Spirit searcheth all things, yea, the deep things of God.

For what man knoweth the things of a man, save the spirit of man which is in him? Even so the things of God knoweth no man, but the Spirit of God. Now we have received, not the spirit of the world, but the spirit which is of God; that we might know the things that are freely given to us of God. Which things also we speak, not in the words which man's wisdom teacheth, but which the Holy Ghost teacheth; comparing spiritual things with spiritual."

Since Paul had so emphatically stated that the Gospel is not based on the wisdom of man, it might perhaps be concluded by some that it therefore contains no wisdom of any kind. The apostle now proceeds to show that there is a higher wisdom than the human—the wisdom of God—and that upon this divine wisdom is the Gospel founded.

Paul insists that we do however "speak wisdom among them that are perfect." The word here translated "perfect" means literally "full grown." It is not synonymous with the term *believer*, for sad to say some believers are not full-grown—3:1 makes this quite clear. It rather describes the sort of person spoken of in 2:15 as "he that is spiritual." The reference then is not to absolute perfection for this no mortal possesses, but to one who is mature, well developed spiritually, in contrast to a "babe."

The apostle explains however that the wisdom of which he speaks is not the "wisdom of this age," nor is it the wisdom of the "rulers of this age," the latter expression referring to men with worldly authority. Despite all their vaunted wisdom these human rulers are "coming to naught," which signifies "the gradual nullification of these 'rulers' before the final and certain triumph of the power of Christ in His kingdom" (A. T. Robertson).

Though the message of the Gospel may be foolishness to men, it is in reality "the wisdom of God," but yet "in a mystery." A New Testament *mystery* is something previously concealed in the counsels of God, or at least not fully revealed, but now made known to men. This divine wisdom of Christ crucified was no mere afterthought or last minute plan on the part of God. Quite the contrary. It was conceived in His eternal mind "before the ages" and then carried out by His sovereign will. All was done "unto our glory." Because of what Christ has accomplished, we —poor sinners that we are—shall receive glory, even as we glorify Him.

The rulers of this world, depending solely on human wisdom, had no conception of this divine plan of God. This is clearly demonstrated by the fact that instead of receiving the Lord of glory when He came to this earth, they rejected and crucified Him.

In verse 9, the apostle speaks of man's way of acquiring knowledge, a way which is completely inadequate for grasping the wisdom of God. Man has three channels for receiving knowledge: through the "eye gate," through the "ear gate," and through the reasonings of the "heart" (or *mind*). In dealing with purely earthly things, these channels may be fairly satisfactory. They fail completely even to "scratch the surface" when it comes to the things of God. The greatest spiritual realities are unseen to the physical eye, unheard by the physical ear, infinitely beyond the thinking ability of the natural mind. In dealing with this subject, Paul quotes the sense of Isaiah 64:4, though not the exact words. These wonderful, but by human standards unsearchable, things of which the apostle is speaking are the things which God has prepared "for them that love him." They can be learned in only one way—by revelation of God through His Holy Spirit. The point is not that He *will* reveal them some day, but that

He has *already* revealed them to those of us who are Christians, by the work of the Holy Spirit. Certain truths are described as "the deep things of God." In the next chapter the apostle distinguishes between the "milk" and the "meat" of God's Word. Evidently there are some things of God which are comparatively simple and others that are very deep. (Rev. 2:24 indicates that Satan also has his "deep things," things which human beings are better off never to learn.)

A man is able to understand the feelings and problems of other men because he is a like human being, and has had experiences of a similar nature. Conversely however, he is unable to comprehend the reactions of a lower order of being, such as an animal, or of a higher, such as an angel, since he has not the nature of one of these. If this is true, how much more is it to be expected that the natural man is unable to understand anything about an infinite God. The Spirit of God alone is capable of such comprehension. So it is quite logical that if these truths are to be known by man at all, they *must* be revealed by the Spirit.

The "spirit of the world" which Paul affirms that we Christians have *not* received, is the spirit of the natural man with his human wisdom. Believers have been granted the gift of the Holy Spirit, so that He might reveal to them the wonderful spiritual possessions God has given them.

Revelation is presented in verse 10, *illumination* in verse 12, and *inspiration* in verse 13. *We* in the last mentioned verse means "we apostles." The apostles spoke these deep things of God, not in human words, but in words taught by the Holy Spirit. So it is made clear that inspiration extends not only to the thoughts expressed but also to the *words* used to express these concepts. The last phrase of verse 13 is best rendered "adapting spiritual words to spiritual truths" (Weymouth).

F. Men's Condition Is Made Clear by Their Reception of God's Wisdom (2:14-16)

"But the natural man receiveth not the things of the Spirit of God: for they are foolishness unto him: neither can he know them, because they are spiritually discerned. But he that is spiritual judgeth all things, yet he himself is judged of no man. For who hath known the mind of the Lord, that he may instruct him? But we have the mind of Christ."

A great class of human beings is unable to receive these wondrous truths of God: "the natural man." This is the unregenerate man in his natural fallen condition. It is not simply that he refuses to receive these things. He actually considers them foolishness. It is difficult to realize, but true, that no matter how intelligent he may be he really has no capacity to "know them, because they are spiritually discerned." Even in the purely natural realm, people often consider things to be foolish which they cannot understand. How much more is this true with regard to spiritual matters! Little wonder then that sometimes a man who is highly educated—but unregenerate—will scoff at the things of God.

On the other hand, the man who is born again and spiritually mature discerns and understands even these deep things of God. He himself however is in a realm so remote from that of the natural man, that the latter cannot understand him at all: "he himself is judged of no man."

Chapter 2 closes with a quotation from Isaiah 40:13.

No one is able to teach or instruct the Lord Jehovah. The fact is that the natural man is unable even to comprehend the things of God, nor is he able to understand the spiritual man, who has "the mind of Christ."

G. The Corinthians Are Carnal—Saved But Following Man's Wisdom (3:1-9)

"And I, brethren, could not speak unto you as unto spiritual, but as unto carnal, even as unto babes in Christ. I have fed you with milk, and not with meat: for hitherto ye were not able to bear it, neither yet now are ye able. For ye are yet carnal: for whereas there is among you envying, and strife, and divisions, are ye not carnal, and walk as men? For while one saith, I am of Paul; and another, I am of Apollos; are ye not carnal? Who then is Paul, and who is Apollos, but ministers by whom ye believed, even as the Lord gave to every man? I have planted, Apollos watered; but God gave the increase. So then neither is he that planteth anything, neither he that watereth; but God that giveth the increase. Now he that planteth and he that watereth are one: and every man shall receive his own reward according to his own labor. For we are laborers together with God: ye are God's husbandry, ye are God's building."

In this paragraph the apostle turns to apply the principles just enunciated in the previous chapter. The Corinthian Christians, who should be *spiritual*, are in fact *carnal*, and because of this are little better able to understand the things of God than is the natural man. Therefore the apostle proceeds to accurately diagnose the real underlying cause of the divisions and dissensions in the church at Corinth, as well as in other churches elsewhere (1:2).

There is no doubt about the fact that the Corinthians are truly saved—they are "brethren," they are "babes *in Christ*." But they are not spiritual men and women. Instead they are *carnal*, or *fleshly*. They are born again, but are still allowing the old nature to control them. For this reason Paul has not been able to teach them the "deep things of God." He has rather had to "feed" them with "milk." They were and they still continue to be "baby Christians." "There is no disgrace in being a babe, but prolonged infancy is pitiable, and arrested development is deplorable. Regeneration does not denote moral perfection, but the beginning of a new life. There must be growth from the state of a babe to that of a mature man" (Erdman).

The fact that there are among them *envying, strife,* and *divisions* is proof that they are *carnal* Christians. These things are all manifestations of the flesh. Each of the three is found in the list of the "works of the flesh" in Galatians 5:19, 20, the word rendered *divisions* here, there being translated as *seditions*. What a tragic contrast with the "fruit of the Spirit" in Galatians 5:22, 23! The fact is that the Corinthians are "walking as men"— in other words, living as unregenerate people who do not know the Lord at all. They are grouping themselves around human teachers, then arguing and quarreling with one another. This is carnality. "Arguments that deflect the mind from the centrality of Christ and His cross are fleshly and carnal. They hinder development. They prevent the Church fulfilling its function, and all these things result from the yielding to the flesh, the lower side of the nature. That is the diagnosis and the symptoms that prove it, as Paul saw them in Corinth" (Morgan).

One most important antidote for their sad condition is to be found in a true view of human teachers, such as Paul and Apollos. They are never to be placed upon a pedestal as "popes." They are simply "ministers"—*servants* of God, channels through whom the Word of God has come to the Corinthians, as they used the gifts given to them, "even as the Lord gave to every man" some gift (see I Cor. 12:11). In this case Paul planted the seed, Apollos came along later and "watered." Had not God "given the increase" the work of both would have been useless. The human channels are in themselves nothing— God is everything. Apollos and Paul however "are one." There is no division between them and they never had any intention whatever of raising up parties or cliques around themselves. But, beautifully enough, even though God's servants are in themselves nothing, yet nevertheless each shall some day at the judgment seat of Christ "receive his own reward" in accordance with the diligence and faithfulness with which he has used his abilities and opportunities.

Even leaders such as Apollos and Paul are simply "laborers together with God," or better, "God's fellow-workers" (A.S.V.). "We are not workers with God. That is not the idea the apostle is here setting forth. We are fellow-workers who belong to God, and who are working with one another. As God's servants we have a common task; it is to labor in the field which belongs to God, in the Church, in the tilled land where one has been doing the planting and another the watering; or, suddenly to change the figure of speech, we are fellow-workers engaged in erecting the great temple which is being built for a habitation of God. . . . Such a conception of the Christian ministry will secure unity for the

Church and promote humility and sympathy among the servants of Christ" (Erdman).

H. Building on the True Foundation (3:10-15)

"According to the grace of God which is given unto me, as a wise masterbuilder, I have laid the foundation, and another buildeth thereon. But let every man take heed how he buildeth thereupon. For other foundation can no man lay than that is laid, which is Jesus Christ. Now if any man build upon this foundation gold, silver, precious stones, wood, hay, stubble; every man's work shall be made manifest: for the day shall declare it, because it shall be revealed by fire; and the fire shall try every man's work of what sort it is. If any man's work abide which he hath built thereupon, he shall receive a reward. If any man's work shall be burned, he shall suffer loss: but he himself shall be saved; yet so as by fire."

As a "wise masterbuilder," or *skillful architect,* Paul has been the first to preach the Gospel in Corinth. He has "laid the foundation," so to speak. Thus he continues the picture of the building, the temple. The foundation is Christ. He is the only true foundation on which men can build, whether it be a church or a life. Each builds on that foundation, but different ones build diversely. Some work faithfully, building a good and true life. Others do inferior work. Probably a difference is intended in each of the six things mentioned in verse 12: gold, silver, precious stones, wood, hay, stubble. There is quite evidently a twofold distinction between the first three and the last three items: useful work, and that which is more or less useless. Eventually the labors of every believer will be "made manifest." This will be at the judgment seat of Christ. The work which in that day stands the test of the refining fire will "receive a reward." The man whose labor is worthless and consumed by the fire "will suffer loss." He will not lose his *soul*, but he will lose his *reward*.

I. Warning Against the Destruction of God's Temple (3:16, 17)

"Know ye not that ye are the temple of God, and that the Spirit of God dwelleth in you? If any man defile the temple of God, him shall God destroy; for the temple of God is holy, which temple are ye."

The entire Church is here pictured as God's *temple*. The original word, it is beautiful to note, refers not to the temple as a whole, but to the *holy of holies*. This same figure is used just a little later (6:19) of the individual Christian. In the present context however the thought is that the person who injures or mars this temple—God's Church—shall receive his retribution from God.

J. The Christian's Limitations and Resources (3:18-23)

"Let no man deceive himself. If any man among you seemeth to be wise in this world, let him become a fool, that he may be wise. For the wisdom of this world is foolishness with God. For it is written, He taketh the wise in their own craftiness. And again, The Lord knoweth the thoughts of the wise, that they are vain. Therefore let no man glory in men. For all things are yours; whether Paul, or Apollos, or Cephas, or the world, or life, or death, or things present, or things to come; all are yours; and ye are Christ's; and Christ is God's."

Again the apostle rebukes the Corinthians for their love of worldly wisdom—a love which was producing such unhappy divisions among them. In such matters it is all too easy to be self deceived. Paul suggests that if any man thinks he is wise in the wisdom of this age, then such a one had better become what the world considers a fool. He had better receive with simple, childlike faith the Word of God, for then he will be *truly* wise. With God, the vaunted wisdom of the philosophers of this world is utter and absolute foolishness. The best reasoning of the finest minds is unable to bring man to God and to salvation. To prove this the apostle quotes first Job 5:13 and then Psalm 94:11.

Indeed no Christian should *glory in men.* We must never glorify a human leader and then follow him to the exclusion of all other true teachers of God's Word. It is actually absurd to do so—"all things are yours," says Paul. Every true, godly teacher of the Word is for the benefit of each Christian: *Paul,* with his outstanding Gospel preaching and burning zeal for the Lord; *Apollos* with his surpassing knowledge of the Scriptures and his eloquent presentation of Bible truth; *Peter* with his lovable human personality and bright memories of the personal ministry of the Lord Jesus. Even beyond this, says the apostle, *the world* is yours. All the truly lovely and beautiful things of God's creation are for each of us to enjoy. In all nature the Christian sees the beauty of the great Creator (Rom. 1:20).

> Heav'n above is softer blue,
> Earth around is sweeter green!
> Something lives in every hue
> Christless eyes have never seen:
> Birds with gladder songs o'erflow,

Flow'rs with deeper beauties shine,
Since I know, as now I know,
I am His, and He is mine.
                    —WADE ROBINSON

"Things present"—in other words, present events—are ours. We can rest assured that "all things work together for good to them that love God" (Rom. 8:28). We need not fear the *future*, as it likewise is ours. Life with its trials and problems—even death itself—shall not master the one who walks with Christ: "All are yours." The reason these things are true is because "ye are Christ's," and we know that "Christ is God's."

K. God's Stewards (4:1-5)

"Let a man so account of us, as of the ministers of Christ, and stewards of the mysteries of God. Moreover it is required in stewards, that a man be found faithful. But with me it is a very small thing that I should be judged of you, or of man's judgment: yea, I judge not mine own self. For I know nothing by myself; yet am I not hereby justified: but he that judgeth me is the Lord. Therefore judge nothing before the time, until the Lord come, who both will bring to light the hidden things of darkness, and will make manifest the counsels of the hearts: and then shall every man have praise of God."

Paul has just affirmed that various Christian teachers belong to all the believers—they "are yours." Nevertheless they are not to think that they have the right to rule over such men and order them around in accordance with personal whim. Such men are not "ministers of the church," but rather "ministers of Christ"—*servants* of Christ. The Lord is their master. Ministers are "stewards of the mysteries of God." A *steward* is a person who manages an estate or household, dispensing to other servants their tasks and their provisions. The "mysteries of God" are deep divine truths, hidden from human wisdom, but revealed by God to His own. The most essential quality a steward can have is not brilliance or ability, but *faithfulness*. According to these very qualities of brilliance and ability have the Corinthians been judging their spiritual instructors. These things however are relatively unimportant. And not only have they been following one particular teacher exclusively, but they have unfairly criticized others, Paul included.

The apostle solemnly insists that it matters little to him what the Corinthians think of him. It is even of little concern to him what the age in general thinks of him. His reference to "man's judgment" is literally "of man's day," by which he means the present dispensation or age. Actually it is not even of supreme importance what he thinks of himself, as sad to say human beings are easily self-deceived. So far as he knows himself, Paul states that his conscience is clear (see Acts 23:1), he knows "nothing against myself" (literal rendering of v. 4). But even that is not the final test, as he writes "yet am I not hereby justified." "St. Paul is here using the word in its legal rather than its theological sense" (*Pulpit Commentary*). The final and proper judge is the Lord. He knows all things. When He comes He will judge the acts and motives of all Christians. Then shall each one have the praise which is rightfully due him.

L. The Apostolic Example (4:6-16)

"And these things, brethren, I have in a figure transferred to myself and to Apollos for your sakes; that ye might learn in us not to think of men above that which is written, that no one of you be puffed up for one against another. For who maketh thee to differ from another? and what hast thou that thou didst not receive? now if thou didst receive it, why dost thou glory, as if thou hadst not received it? Now ye are full, now ye are rich, ye have reigned as kings without us: and I would to God ye did reign, that we also might reign with you. For I think that God hath set forth us the apostles last, as it were appointed to death: for we are made a spectacle unto the world, and to angels, and to men. We are fools for Christ's sake, but ye are wise in Christ; we are weak, but ye are strong; ye are honorable, but we are despised. Even unto this present hour we both hunger, and thirst, and are naked, and are buffeted, and have no certain dwellingplace; and labor, working with our own hands: being reviled, we bless; being persecuted, we suffer it: being defamed, we intreat: we are made as the filth of the world, and are the offscouring of all things unto this day. I write not these things to shame you, but as my beloved sons I warn you. For though ye have ten thousand instructors in Christ, yet have ye not many fathers: for in Christ Jesus I have begotten you through the gospel. Wherefore I beseech you, be ye followers of me."

The apostle, with this paragraph, draws to a conclusion his discussion of divisions. He says: "Now these considerations, brethren, I have specially applied to Apollos and myself" (Weymouth's translation). He has not undertaken to name all the teachers around whom the Corinthians have been grouping themselves, but has rather used himself and Apollos as examples. However the truths taught apply to all. Christians are not to think of human beings "above that which is written." We must not go beyond the general teaching of Scripture on this subject. By going further in this than the Word of God authorizes, the Corinthians have become "puffed up" and quarrelsome. The actual cause of these divisions is their own pride. Therefore the apostle reminds them that any good gifts or abilities they may have are from the Lord. They should then be the ground of gratitude not of human pride.

Verse 8 is evidently satirical. Puffed up by their human wisdom and pride, these people imagine themselves as *full, rich, reigning like kings.* All this is but pitiful delusion. Paul expresses the fervent wish that it was *really* true, that the day had come when all of us *will* reign with Christ. But that remains for His glorious return and millennial kingdom. With true apostles suffering as they do now, how can their followers expect to be honored and glorified by the world, as the Corinthians seemed to think they should be?

Paul's allusion in verse 9 seems to be to condemned criminals who were brought out last in the great Roman spectacles, to fight unarmed with wild beasts, having no hope because they were "appointed to death." The apostles are willing to be considered "fools" for Christ's sake, to be weak and despised. The Corinthians on the contrary, consider themselves wise and strong, deserving of honor in the world. In verses 11-13 Paul speaks at length of the sufferings of the apostles. In spite of these trials they "bless" and "intreat."

Paul makes it clear that he is not writing just to shame the Corinthians. It is rather because they are his beloved spiritual children, and he wishes to warn them of a course which in the end can only result in trouble and misery for themselves. While they may have had many good teachers, he himself bears to them a unique relationship. He was the first one who preached the Gospel to them, the first to lead them to Christ. As their spiritual "father" he very naturally entreats them to follow his own example of humility and unselfish service to Christ.

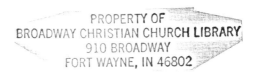

Chapter Four

ERRORS CORRECTED:
IMMORALITY
(4:17—6:20)

A. Godly Life the Test of Profession (4:17-21)

FOR THIS CAUSE have I sent unto you Timotheus, who is my beloved son, and faithful in the Lord, who shall bring you into remembrance of my ways which be in Christ, as I teach everywhere in every church. Now some are puffed up, as though I would not come to you. But I will come to you shortly, if the Lord will, and will know, not the speech of them which are puffed up, but the power. For the kingdom of God is not in word, but in power. What will ye? shall I come unto you with a rod, or in love, and in the spirit of meekness?"

As spiritual father to the Corinthian church, Paul has sent his beloved helper Timothy to remind the people once more of the practice and teaching of the apostle himself. They are not however to think by this that he is not going to pay them a personal visit. He does not wish his critics to become puffed up, imagining Paul is afraid to face them. It is his intention to come himself at an early date. Then he will discover whether those who are puffed up with pride are really demonstrating the

power of God in their lives, as they claim. His approach
at this future visit will depend on the manner in which
they now heed his written warnings. If they refuse to
listen, if they continue on in their unscriptural way, he
will be forced to deal with them severely (cf. II Cor.
13:10). On the other hand, if they show their good faith
by changing their wrong ways, then he will come "in
love, and in the spirit of meekness."

B. "Purge Out the Old Leaven" (5:1-8)

"It is reported commonly that there is fornication
among you, and such fornication as is not so much as
named among the Gentiles, that one should have his
father's wife. And ye are puffed up, and have not rather
mourned, that he that hath done this deed might be taken
away from among you. For I verily, as absent in body,
but present in spirit, have judged already, as though I
were present concerning him that hath so done this deed,
in the name of our Lord Jesus Christ, when ye are
gathered together, and my spirit, with the power of our
Lord Jesus Christ, to deliver such an one unto Satan for
the destruction of the flesh, that the spirit may be saved
in the day of the Lord Jesus. Your glorying is not good.
Know ye not that a little leaven leaveneth the whole
lump? Purge out therefore the old leaven, that ye may be
a new lump, as ye are unleavened. For even Christ our
passover is sacrificed for us: therefore let us keep the
feast, not with old leaven, neither with the leaven of
malice and wickedness; but with the unleavened bread
of sincerity and truth."

It is common knowledge that the Corinthians are not
demonstrating the power of God by godly lives. A most

flagrant example of incest is mentioned. One of their number is living in immoral relations with his step-mother. Even Gentiles—godless unsaved people—would turn in shame from such a sin. Yet the Corinthians, who know of this, are not mourning over the matter but are rather puffed up. It hardly seems that they could have been proud of such a sin. Paul's meaning probably is either that they were proud of their divisions and engrossed with such matters consequently overlooking this evil, or that they were proud of themselves for being broadminded, as they thought, and therefore deemed it a commendable thing to ignore this act of gross immorality.

Though not present in person, Paul has "in spirit" judged with them the one guilty of this unrighteous act as deserving to be put out of the church—in other words, excommunicated. Since this man has willingly submitted himself to Satan, he is to be turned out into Satan's realm "for the destruction of the flesh." Some expositors understand this expression to refer to bodily disease being inflicted on the sinning person, but it should be noted that the word used is not *body* but *flesh*. Paul's thought seems to be that, cut off from any fellowship with true Christians and handed over completely to the flesh, the backsliding brother will eventually sicken of the flesh-life, and turn from it, that is, if he is truly a saved person.

Another reason is advanced as to why their "glorying" in the face of such a sin "is not good." Just as a little leaven will corrupt and leaven over a whole mass of dough, so sin tolerated in the church (or in the individual life) has an insidious way of growing. The old leaven must be purged out. To make this warning more impressive, the apostle uses in their typical meaning two of the Old Testament feasts of Israel. The first feast of the Jews' religious year was the Passover, which was to be celebrated on the fourteenth day of the first month. Immediately following, for the next seven days, was the feast of unleavened bread. During these days no leaven whatsoever was to be used or even kept in the homes. Now *leaven* in Scripture always typifies evil—false doctrine, false principles of life. Paul states that for us, in this New Testament age, the Passover is Christ. Our new life begins when we believe on Him and are cleansed by His blood. This cleansing should be followed in a spiritual way by the "feast of unleavened bread"—a separated walk, or life, on the part of the redeemed one. This means turning away from the old life of malice and wickedness to the new life in Christ of sincerity and truth.

C. Christian Fellowship Limited (5:9-13)

"I wrote unto you in an epistle not to company with fornicators: yet not altogether with the fornicators of this world, or with the covetous, or extortioners, or with idolaters; for then must ye needs go out of the world. But now have I written unto you not to keep company, if any man that is called a brother be a fornicator, or covetous, or an idolater, or a railer, or a drunkard, or an extortioner; with such an one no not to eat. For what have I to do to judge them also that are without? do not ye judge them that are within? But them that are without God judgeth. Therefore put away from among yourselves that wicked person."

It is evident that in some previous communication the apostle had advised the Corinthians not to have fellowship with fornicators, such as the man just mentioned in the opening of chapter 5. The Corinthians apparently misunderstood this injunction however, thinking Paul meant they were to have nothing whatsoever to do with even unsaved people who were guilty of such immorality. The apostle shows that he did not by his previous instruction mean that they should have no contact at all with unsaved people who were guilty of such sins as fornication, covetousness, idolatry, or extortion. What he actually meant was that if a *Christian brother* is guilty of such gross sins he should be excluded from Christian fellowship. With such a one believers should not eat—either at the Lord's Supper, or anywhere else. It is not the duty of believers to attempt to straighten out all the errors in the lives of unsaved people (note in this connection Luke 12:13, 14). *But* those who are "within"—and by this is meant *within* the church—should be disciplined by the church and removed from fellowship if living in wickedness. Those outside the church we can safely and entirely leave in the hands of God.

D. Christians Warned Against Going to Law (6:1-11)

"Dare any of you, having a matter against another, go to law before the unjust, and not before the saints? Do ye not know that the saints shall judge the world? and if the world shall be judged by you, are ye unworthy to judge the smallest matters? Know ye not that we shall judge angels? how much more things that pertain to this life? If then ye have judgments of things pertaining to this life, set them to judge who are least esteemed in the church. I speak to your shame. Is it so, that there is not a wise man among you? no, not one that shall be able to judge between his brethren? But brother goeth to law with brother, and that before the unbelievers. Now therefore there is utterly a fault among you, because ye go to law one with another. Why do ye not rather take wrong? why do ye not rather suffer yourselves to be defrauded? Nay, ye do wrong, and defraud, and that your brethren. Know ye not that the unrighteous shall not inherit the kingdom of God? Be not deceived: neither fornicators, nor idolaters, nor adulterers, nor effeminate, nor abusers of themselves with mankind, nor thieves, nor covetous, nor drunkards, nor revilers, nor extortioners, shall inherit the kingdom of God. And such were some of you: but ye are washed, but ye are sanctified, but ye are justified in the name of the Lord Jesus, and by the Spirit of our God."

While on one hand the Corinthians were careless about serious sins such as the one just discussed in the opening part of the previous chapter, yet at the same time they were quick to go to law with one another in civil courts, and that over petty grievances they should have easily settled for themselves. Paul expresses amazement at their audacity in doing such a thing. He is astonished that Christians should go to law with other Christians before unsaved judges. He argues that in view of the fact that believers will one day have a part in the judgment of men and angels, how much more should they now be able to judge small matters among themselves. It should be added that this does not forbid Christians using the courts on occasion to secure justice. This can be seen by comparing the experience of Paul himself in Acts 25:10, 11, and his further teaching on the subject in Romans 13:1-4. The reference in I Corinthians 6 is to Christians disputing among themselves over petty matters.

Verse 4 is better rendered (as in the A.S.V.) by a question: "If then ye have judgments of things pertaining

to this life, do ye set them to judge who are least esteemed in the church?" The point is, if you were going to
seek a judgment on some question would you look to the
least respected of Christians for it? If you would not think
of doing this, how much less then should you look to an
unsaved judge. This, Paul states, is "utterly a fault." The
A.S.V. uses the word *defect*. It is a "loss" in a spiritual
way that such things should happen among God's people.
The apostle affirms that it would be better to endure
wrong, to be defrauded, than to be always running to
heathen courts. But the sad fact is that the people re-
sponsible for this are not actually seeking justice but are
rather trying to defraud others, and these even their very
brethren in Christ.

The word rendered "unjust" in verse 1 is translated
"unrighteous" in verse 9. Such will not inherit the kingdom of God, being characterized in verses 9 and 10 by
a list of fearful sins. This does not at all mean to say that
people who have ever been guilty of such sins can never
be saved. Quite the contrary—Paul says of the Corinthian
Christians—"such were some of you." But when they received Christ as Saviour, they, like all other believers
then or now, were washed from their sins, were sanctified,
were justified. If God has forgiven them so much, then
why should not they in turn forgive their brethren in the
petty disputes just mentioned? Christ's teaching in Matthew 18:21-35 is very much to the point here.

E. The Highest Appeal for Purity (6:12-20)

"All things are lawful unto me, but all things are not
expedient: all things are lawful for me, but I will not be
brought under the power of any. Meats for the belly, and

the belly for meats: but God shall destroy both it and them. Now the body is not for fornication, but for the Lord; and the Lord is for the body. And God hath both raised up the Lord, and will also raise up us by his own power. Know ye not that your bodies are the members of Christ? shall I then take the members of Christ, and make them the members of an harlot? God forbid. What? know ye not that he which is joined to an harlot is one body? for two, saith he, shall be one flesh. But he that is joined unto the Lord is one spirit. Flee fornication. Every sin that a man doeth is without the body; but he that committeth fornication sinneth against his own body. What? know ye not that your body is the temple of the Holy Ghost which is in you, which ye have of God, and ye are not your own? For ye are bought with a price: therefore glorify God in your body, and in your spirit, which are God's."

With these words the apostle takes up once more the question of sexual immorality, a sin notoriously prevalent in the city of Corinth. It is possible that certain of the Corinthians had been using the teaching of Paul that we are not under law but under grace as a means of justifying their immoral actions. Such an attitude is sometimes called *antinomianism*. The apostle shows that it is not a question of the *law* at all, but rather of what is *expedient*, or better, according to modern usage, *profitable*. As saved people, we belong to Christ and to Christ alone. We must not be brought under the power (or *authority*) of *any other thing*. This is true even of things which may seem harmless in themselves. How much more is it applicable to that which is actually impure or immoral. And with such Paul will shortly deal very specifically.

It is possible for a person to become a "slave," so to

speak, to his own stomach, and live solely to gratify his physical appetite. Now, as the apostle shows, there is certainly nothing wrong with putting food in the belly—it was made for this very purpose. But it must always be remembered that this is not the whole end of life—both the belly and the food in it will eventually turn to dust.

But whereas the body was made to partake of food, it was *not* created for fornication. God never intended that human beings should live in impurity and sin. Instead the body was made to be a clean instrument for the Lord's use. Wonderful indeed is the statement that "the Lord [was made] for the body." The Lord Jesus Christ became flesh and took on a body such as ours that He might redeem our mortal bodies. After His body had passed through death for us, He was raised up by God who will also raise us up too, some day, to a glorified body. In view of this we should even now keep our bodies pure.

At the time we were saved, we were united with Christ, made one with Him. Our own bodies are now considered to be the same as His—we are "the members of Christ." It would be altogether unthinkable to take that which belongs to Christ and use it for immoral purposes. Sexual sin was common in Corinth in connection with the heathen worship of the goddess Venus. Evidently some of the Corinthian Christians had still not realized that if they had sexual relations with a prostitute, that would be uniting with such a person even as in the true marriage relationship, which was instituted in the beginning by God. Since Christians have been spiritually united with Christ, to be "joined to an harlot" would be disloyalty and treason to Him.

The apostle solemnly warns all of us to "flee" such a sin, even as Joseph fled the solicitations of the wife of

Potiphar. In matters where the passions are easily aroused it is dangerous folly to "play with fire." From such sins Christians should stay as far away as possible. There are other sins, such as theft for example, which although quite wrong do not in themselves harm the body of the sinner. Sexual sin differs in that it is indeed a sin against one's own body, being often the cause of diseases which weaken and destroy the physical system.

Still further appeals are made by Paul for purity of life: the body of the Christian is the *temple of the Holy Spirit* and ought to be kept clean for Him. Actually the body of the believer does not belong to him—it belongs to Christ who has bought each of us "with a price." So in both a physical and a spiritual way, the Christian should seek to glorify God.

Chapter Five

ERRORS CORRECTED:
CONCERNING MARRIAGE
(7:1-40)

A. Responsibilities of Marriage (7:1-7)

N OW CONCERNING THE THINGS whereof ye wrote unto
me: It is good for a man not to touch a woman.
Nevertheless, to avoid fornication, let every man have
his own wife, and let every woman have her own husband. Let the husband render unto the wife due benevolence: and likewise also the wife unto the husband. The
wife hath not power of her own body, but the husband:
and likewise also the husband hath not power of his own
body, but the wife. Defraud ye not one the other, except
it be with consent for a time, that ye may give yourselves
to fasting and prayer; and come together again, that
Satan tempt you not for your incontinency. But I speak
this by permission, and not of commandment. For I
would that all men were even as I myself. But every man
hath his proper gift of God, one after this manner, and
another after that."

Sad to say, this present chapter of I Corinthians has
been grossly misunderstood. Because of certain state-
ments contained in it, Paul has been pictured by critics

as a narrow ascetic, a warped and twisted man who hated women and despised marriage. Such a conclusion is utterly unwarranted. Two facts need to be kept firmly in mind: (1) The apostle is not here dealing with the subject of marriage in general, but is specifically answering direct questions the Corinthians had previously addressed to him, questions which we do not now have before us. Furthermore, these questions pertained to local problems with which we are not thoroughly familiar at the present day. "No attempt is made to state the Christian doctrine of marriage in its fullness and completeness. That must be sought elsewhere, and will be found if we study his Ephesian and Colossian letters, and those to Timothy. There we have specific instructions on the marriage relationship. Here it looks as though Paul considered the marriage state a little lower than the state of celibacy. However, he cannot be interpreted in that way, for do not forget that when he was writing to Timothy he spoke of 'forbidding to marry' as a 'doctrine of demons'" (G. Campbell Morgan).

(2) It must further be considered that the instructions Paul gives in this chapter were in the light of special conditions existing at that time and place (see 7:26). These instructions are not necessarily directly applicable everywhere and every time, though the teachings are of course based on great underlying principles which are always true.

It should be carefully observed that the opening statement of the chapter is *not* that it is *better* for a man to remain unmarried, but that it is *good*. This shows that Paul is not actually comparing the unmarried condition with the married, but is simply affirming that the unmarried state is good and honorable. It may well be that then, as now, there were those who insisted that every person *ought* to marry. Christ's own teaching in Matthew 19:11, 12 proves that such an extreme position is not justified.

Paul immediately asserts however that if there is any danger of the unmarried state tempting a person to satisfy bodily desires by illicit sexual practices, then it is much better to marry. In marriage the apostle insists, it should be noted, on *monogamy*. Each is to have *his own wife* or *her own husband*.

In true marriage there are not only joys but also responsibilities. When a person chooses to enter such a condition, then he or she should be prepared to assume these responsibilities. Mentioned first with regard to such obligations is a matter not of action but of *attitude*. Wife and husband are to render to each other *due benevolence*. The particular Greek word of which this expresison is the translation is used elsewhere in the New Testament only in Ephesians 6:7 where it is rendered "good will." This injunction forbids things which husbands and wives, sad to say, are frequently guilty of: rudeness, innuendo, sarcasm, quarreling, indirect accusations.

It would seem that some in Corinth held the opinion that it was better for those who were married to separate and not to live together as husband and wife. Paul makes it very clear that such is not the case. It is permissible for husbands and wives to separate for short periods of prayer and fasting if they wish. Such times should not be prolonged however lest any might through lack of self-control be led into sin.

Paul's statement of verse 6 is not at all to be understood as though he were here disclaiming inspiration. He simply means that Christians are not *commanded* to marry, but are *permitted* so to do if they wish. Paul expresses his own satisfaction with the unmarried state which, for reasons soon to be given, he could desire that all men were able to share. However he is exceedingly quick to add that the unmarried state is not for all. It is a matter of a special *gift* from God—some have the gift to be married and serve the Lord best in that condition, others to remain single and serve God in that state.

B. Instructions to the Married (7:8-24)

"I say therefore to the unmarried and widows, It is good for them if they abide even as I. But if they cannot contain, let them marry: for it is better to marry than to burn. And unto the married I command, yet not I, but the Lord, Let not the wife depart from her husband: but and if she depart, let her remain unmarried, or be reconciled to her husband: and let not the husband put away his wife. But to the rest speak I, not the Lord: If any brother hath a wife that believeth not, and she be pleased to dwell with him, let him not put her away. And the woman which hath a husband that believeth not, and if he be pleased to dwell with her, let her not leave him. For the unbelieving husband is sanctified by the wife, and the unbelieving wife is sanctified by the husband: else were your children unclean; but now are they holy. But if the unbelieving depart, let him depart. A brother or a sister is not under bondage in such cases: but God hath called us to peace. For what knowest thou, O wife, whether thou shalt save thy husband? or how knowest thou, O man, whether thou shalt save thy wife? But as God hath distributed to every man, as the Lord hath called everyone, so let him walk. And so ordain I in all churches. Is any man called being circumcised? let him not become uncircumcised. Is any called in uncircumcision? let him not be circumcised. Circumcision is nothing, and uncircumcision is nothing, but the keeping of the commandments of God. Let every man abide in the same calling wherein he was called. Art thou called being a servant? care not for it: but if thou mayest be made free, use it rather. For he that is called in the Lord, being a servant, is the Lord's freeman: likewise also he that is called, being free, is Christ's servant. Ye are bought with a price; be not ye the servants of men. Brethren, let every man, wherein he is called, therein abide with God."

With regard to those who are unmarried, or those who have been married but have lost their partners, the apostle affirms that it is better for them to remain in their unmarried state. However if they cannot control their sexual impulses, it is better to marry than to burn with lust. The reason why this is true should be obvious: marriage is good and honorable (Heb. 13:4), while lust is sinful and dishonorable (Matt. 5:28).

While those who are unmarried have *permission* to marry if they so desire, those married are *commanded* not to separate. In extreme cases where they simply cannot get along together and therefore part, they are not to remarry, but to live alone or if possible be reconciled. When the apostle says: "I command, yet not I, but the Lord," he means that not only he himself but also Jesus Christ explicitly commanded this during His earthly ministry. The command of the Lord on this matter is to be found in such passages as Matthew 10:11, 12; 5:32; 19:6; Luke 16:18.

The expression "but to the rest" (v. 12) makes it clear that the above instructions were for cases where both husband and wife were Christians. Now the apostle speaks of the situation where, after marriage, one becomes saved and the other is not. Does that make it permissible for the converted one to leave the unconverted? Absolutely no. The believer should continue to live in the marriage union if the other partner is willing to do so. When in this verse Paul says, "Speak I, not the Lord," he is not by any means disclaiming inspiration. He is rather affirming that on this particular point the Lord, when here on earth, gave no direct teaching. But as an inspired apostle, Paul gives his doctrine on the subject. And a little later he says: "I think also that I have the Spirit of God" (v. 40).

In ancient Israel, if a Jew married a pagan, the union was unholy, and he was ordered to put such a wife away. Also the children of that sort of marriage were considered unholy. For the proof of this, read Ezra 9 and 10. This no longer holds true in this present age of grace. Now "the unbelieving husband is sanctified by the wife" and vice versa. The children, instead of being unclean, are *holy*. Now obviously this does not mean that the faith of a Christian wife can save an unbelieving husband or children. It rather signifies that the believer is to exert a sanctifying influence in the home on the rest of the family, and perhaps in this way bring them to Christ.

If in a mixed marriage, the unbeliever utterly refuses to live with the Christian husband or wife, then the saved one is not obligated to continue on. The statement here does not seem to give specific permission for the believer in such a case to remarry, unless the partner has committed or does commit adultery. But we can be sure that

in this as in all matters "God hath called us to peace"—
it is the Christian's duty always to do that which will produce *peace* rather than strife.

The reason given as to why the believer if possible
should continue to live with the unbeliever is that by this
means the non-Christian may be saved. This teaching
does not however justify one who is a Christian in marry-
ing an unsaved person with the pious hope of later leading that one to the Lord.

After enunciating these important precepts regarding
the marriage union, the apostle proceeds to a general
principle that would apply to any state, either social or
political, in which a person might find himself at the time
of conversion—with the understanding of course that the
condition was honorable. The one who is a Jew is not to
seek to "gentilize" himself, so to speak. The Gentile is not
to attempt to transform himself into a Jew. Actually both
circumcision and uncircumcision are in themselves of no
spiritual significance. The thing of importance is obeying
the moral precepts of God. The one who is a slave is not
to fret about his situation but in it to witness for Christ.
At the same time, Paul hastens to say, if such a one is
offered his freedom he is to take it and use the opportunity for the Lord. Although a slave, a Christian is truly
free in the Lord. If he is a free man, the Christian is
nevertheless a *slave*—the slave of Christ. The fact is that
the believer belongs to Christ. Therefore he should not
make himself the willing slave of any human being. Since
there is little possibility of a person willingly enslaving
himself in a literal sense, doubtless this teaching finds its
primary application in the figurative sense. Summing it
all up, the apostle teaches that each one is to abide in the
condition in which he was saved—"abide with God." This

of course is to continue until and when God may call him to some new situation in life.

C. Advice to the Single and the Married (7:25-40)

"Now concerning virgins I have no commandment of the Lord: yet I give my judgment, as one that hath obtained mercy of the Lord to be faithful. I suppose therefore that this is good for the present distress, I say, that it is good for a man so to be. Art thou bound unto a wife? seek not to be loosed. Art thou loosed from a wife? seek not a wife. But and if thou marry, thou hast not sinned; and if a virgin marry, she hath not sinned. Nevertheless such shall have trouble in the flesh: but I spare you. But this I say, brethren, the time is short: it remaineth, that both they that have wives be as though they had none; and they that weep, as though they wept not; and they that rejoice, as though they rejoiced not; and they that buy, as though they possessed not; and they that use this world, as not abusing it: for the fashion of this world passeth away. But I would have you without carefulness. He that is unmarried careth for the things that belong to the Lord, how he may please the Lord: but he that is married careth for the things of the world, how he may please his wife. There is difference also between a wife and a virgin. The unmarried woman careth for the things of the Lord, that she may be holy both in body and in spirit: but she that is married careth for the things of the world, how she may please her husband. And this I speak for your own profit; not that I may cast a snare upon you, but for that which is comely, and that ye may attend upon the Lord without distraction. But if any man think that he behaveth himself uncomely toward his virgin, if she pass the flower of her age, and need so require, let him do what he will, he sinneth not: let them marry. Nevertheless he that standeth steadfast in his heart, having no necessity, but hath power over his own will, and hath so decreed in his heart that he will keep his virgin, doeth well. So then he that giveth her in marriage doeth well; but he that giveth her not in marriage doeth better. The wife is bound by the law as long as her husband liveth; but if her husband be dead, she is at liberty to be married to whom she will; only in the Lord. But she is happier if she so abide, after my judgment: and I think also that I have the Spirit of God."

In this passage the word *virgins* (v. 25) refers to young unmarried women. The American Revised Version adds the word "daughter" in verses 36, 37, and 38. From Paul's expression, "now concerning virgins," it would seem that certain Christian parents in Corinth were not sure whether to give their daughters in marriage or not. Therefore they had addressed an inquiry to the apostle regarding this matter. Once more he affirms that he has no direct command from the earthly ministry of Christ which he can quote. However he gives his "judgment" (that is *counsel* or *advice*) as from one who must faithfully present the Word of God. Since what he has to say applies equally to both sexes, he first mentions the man (v. 26). Again he says it is good for a man to remain single "for the present distress." This phrase directly refers to local conditions. The Corinthian Christians were facing difficult times of oppression and persecution. Already there had been martyrs for the faith and others would shortly follow in their train. In view of this, the one who has a wife is not to leave her; the one who has none is not to "seek a wife." Undoubtedly this is still a good principle. The person who is anxious to marry and rushes into the first possibility that offers usually makes a mistake!

The man or woman who does marry, however, has committed no sin (v. 28). But such will have "trouble in the flesh." Those who might be tempted lightly to rush into the relationship should consider the fact that there is difficulty, hardship, and grief in the lives of most married couples.

All need to be reminded that the "time is short." This is true of both the individual life and of the age as a whole. There are all too few moments to live and witness for Christ. Nothing then must stand in the way of whole-hearted devotion to Him. In this connection five necessary things are mentioned which are to be found in the lives of most Christians—marriage, sorrow, joy, commerce, material things. In regard to marriage, Paul does not of course mean that husbands should run around with other women and neglect their own wives "as though they had none." Neither does he mean in his remark about "weeping" that Christians should be callously unconcerned at the grief of their friends. What he *does* mean is that none of these five things are to come in between us and the Lord. These matters must not completely occupy our thoughts. We must not become altogether absorbed in this, because the things of earth are passing away.

Further reasons are given as to why the apostle believes the single state to be good for the Christian who has the gift for it. The earnest Christian who is single can devote his time to the Lord alone. The one who is married has an obligation to please his wife. The one who does not provide for his own household is worse than an infidel (I Tim. 5:8). So necessarily the married man or

woman must be more occupied with earthly affairs than
one who is single. This is especially true if there are
children in the family. "He implies that the married
woman must of necessity be more of a Martha than a
Mary" (*Pulpit Commentary*). However these facts are not
brought out to frighten people away from marriage, if
that is their calling. That would be to "cast a snare upon
you" (v. 35). Paul simply wants all Christians to do that
which is *comely* (or *seemly*).

In verses 36-38 the apostle deals specifically with the
question previously mentioned concerning the unmarried
daughters of Christians. If the daughter is fully old
enough to know her own mind, if there are attachments
and commitments, the father does not sin in letting her
marry her sweetheart. It must be remembered that in that
day and country, as well as in many lands now, marriages
were arranged by the parent even though the daughter
was not in love, or actually opposed the union. So Paul
states that the father whose daughter has no desire to
wed—"having no necessity"—does well not to force her
to marry but to allow her to remain single. His conclusion
once again is that the one who gives his daughter in
marriage has committed no sin, but instead "doeth well."
On the other hand, due to "the present distress," he feels
that there are advantages in the single state.

One other type of case is dealt with before the subject
is brought to a close—the woman whose husband has died
—the widow. It should be observed that the reference has
nothing to do with what we call "grass widows" but concerns one whose husband is actually dead. For such a
person it is made quite plain that there is no ban on
second marriages. One stipulation is however made—she
can marry "only in the Lord." This means not merely that

the one she marries must be a Christian, but also that the union should be the definite leading of the Lord, and in His will. While freely permitting such marriages, the apostle offers his counsel that the widow will be better off to remain unmarried.

Chapter Six

ERRORS CORRECTED:
CONCERNING CHRISTIAN LIBERTY
(8—11)

A. Regarding Idols and Meat Offered to Them (8:1-13)

NOW AS TOUCHING THINGS offered unto idols, we know
that we all have knowledge. Knowledge puffeth up,
but charity edifieth. And if any man think that he knoweth anything, he knoweth nothing yet as he ought to
know. But if any man love God, the same is known of
him. As concerning therefore the eating of those things
that are offered in sacrifice unto idols, we know that an
idol is nothing in the world, and that there is none other
God but one. For though there be that are called gods,
whether in heaven or in earth, (as there be gods many,
and lords many,) but to us there is but one God, the
Father, of whom are all things, and we in him; and one
Lord Jesus Christ, by whom are all things, and we by
him. Howbeit there is not in every man that knowledge:
for some with conscience of the idol unto this hour eat
it as a thing offered unto an idol; and their conscience
being weak is defiled. But meat commendeth us not to
God: for neither, if we eat, are we the better; neither, if
we eat not, are we the worse. But take heed lest by any

means this liberty of yours become a stumbling block to them that are weak. For if any man see thee which hast knowledge sit at meat in the idol's temple, shall not the conscience of him which is weak be emboldened to eat those things which are offered to idols; and through thy knowledge shall the weak brother perish, for whom Christ died? But when ye sin so against the brethren, and wound their weak conscience, ye sin against Christ. Wherefore, if meat make my brother to offend, I will eat no flesh while the world standeth, lest I make my brother to offend."

What is the proper Christian attitude toward things harmless in themselves but with an evil connotation to others? In Corinth, as in other ancient cities, animals were offered in sacrifice, certain parts consumed, then the balance was placed on the market for sale to the public. It is said that this meat was sometimes sold at less than the ordinary price, making it especially attractive to the poor. Among the Corinthian Christians there was evidently considerable difference of opinion as to whether believers should or should not partake of such meat. A question was therefore addressed to the apostle on this subject. In its original form this matter still confronts Christians in certain pagan lands. Although in other countries, like the United States of America, the problem is not directly presented, the *principles* Paul enunciates, being eternally true, are applicable to other questions of a similar nature with which the Christian must deal. "Such are the questions of conscience which confront Christians today: to some they seem to be matters of moral indifference; to others they involve serious questions of right and wrong. Such are the problems relating to the forms of Sabbath observance, to social amusements, to personal expenditures and indulgences" (Erdman).

As a starting principle, it is stated that "we know that we all have knowledge." This manifestly does not mean that all Christians know everything there is to be known. It rather means that all true Christians have knowledge about certain basic facts. One such fact is stated in verse 4. So we all have knowledge of certain essential truths, and can act upon these. If we acted upon knowledge alone, we would eat such meat. However we cannot proceed upon knowledge alone. Knowledge by itself tends to "puff up" a person. It must therefore be seasoned with *love* (rendered *charity* in the Authorized Version). Love "builds up" (or *edifies*).

If any man thinks he knows something perfectly, then he really doesn't know anything as he should. One theologian has defined *knowledge* as "passing from a state of unconscious ignorance to a state of conscious ignorance" (Chafer). Of one thing we can however be certain: love is better than knowledge. If a person truly loves God, He knows it and will in such a case excuse small mistakes committed through ignorance.

Paul sums up that which *knowledge* can teach us on the particular subject in hand. We know that an idol—an image of stick or stone—is actually nothing at all. We know there is but one God. We know that though there are many called "gods" in this world, there is really but one God—our heavenly Father. Though many are called lords, we know that we have but One—the Lord Jesus Christ. We know that of our God "are all things." This refers to the *old* creation. We know that we are "in him." This is the *new* creation. We know that by Christ "are all things" (old creation) and "we by him" (new creation).

Sad to say, however, "there is not in every man that knowledge." Some, while knowing theoretically that an idol is nothing, are yet unable fully to break away from old associations in which they thought of these idols as evil deities. If they should eat meat that had been offered to idols they would feel that they had committed a sin and "their conscience being weak is defiled."

In such words Paul plainly intimates that there is really nothing actually wrong with eating such meat, and has spoken of the one who feels defiled by it as having a "weak conscience." In verse 8 he clearly states that meat really has nothing to do one way or the other with our standing before God. If we eat we are not "better." If we refrain from eating we are not "worse." The whole thing is purely a matter of personal choice.

In matters which are immaterial in themselves, such as this, the Christian has liberty to do as he pleases. However not just knowledge alone must be taken into account but also love. The believer must be careful lest by a certain action which in itself is not wrong he nevertheless should put a stumbling block before weaker brethren. As a practical example, Paul suggests an extreme case. Whether the situation he mentions actually took place is problematical but anyhow it serves as a good illustration. A Christian with knowledge goes so far as to attend a feast at a pagan temple. A weak believer—that is, one who does not fully understand the scriptural principles of right and wrong—sees this and is led by the example of the stronger person to violate his own conscience so as to do what he thinks is wrong. This brother, "for whom Christ died" even as He did for the stronger Christian, thus goes against conscience and begins a downward course that eventually ends in the complete destruction of his testimony for Christ. If such is the outcome, an act possibly neither right nor wrong in itself becomes a definite sin. And this sin is not simply against a human brother, but against Christ Himself.

For the moment Paul ends his discussion of the matter by stating the great principle he himself follows. Surely it is one by which every true Christian should live. *If* it caused his brother to stumble, he would be willing to give up anything, not just meat offered to idols, but meat itself. The true Christian standard should be to totally abstain from that which is *evil*, and to refrain also from anything else *if* it would be a stumbling block to others.

One item of caution may well be added in the cogent words of G. Campbell Morgan: "I have heard of unjustifiable and unwarranted use made of that statement. We must remember this must be interpreted by a justifiable effect of conscience on our action, and no further. I do not think any particular word of application is necessary. It must be proved that an example of ours ever made anyone to stumble, or offend in that particular matter. That applies in a good many ways. Some people make use of it when there is no excuse for their action, when it is not based upon our action. . . . I do not suppose anyone would dream of saying, 'If clothes maketh my brother to stumble. . . .' You finish it!"

B. Liberty in the Ministry (9:1-23)

1. *Paul's True Apostleship* (9:1-6)

"Am I not an apostle? am I not free? have I not seen Jesus Christ our Lord? are not ye my work in the Lord?

If I be not an apostle unto others, yet doubtless I am to you: for the seal of mine apostleship are ye in the Lord. Mine answer to them that do examine me is this, Have we not power to eat and to drink? Have we not power to lead about a sister, a wife, as well as other apostles, and as the brethren of the Lord, and Cephas? Or I only and Barnabas, have not we power to forbear working?"

Paul continues to deal with the matter of Christian liberty, introduced by the Corinthians' questions as to the eating of meat offered to idols. Eventually he returns to the original subject (10:25) but meantime he offers further illustrations of the principle of foregoing that which one has the *liberty* to take, or even the *right* to take, because of an adverse effect upon others.

In various localities, opponents questioned Paul's apostleship. This was done with the motive of destroying confidence in his authority and thus tearing down his teaching. Since such criticism directly affected the revelation of God which he preached, Paul was forced on a number of occasions to defend his apostleship. In Corinth, false teachers had accused him of not accepting money from the people because he knew in his heart that he was an impostor. Now the time has come to demonstrate his rights as an apostle. Later in the chapter he will explain why he did not claim those rights but was willing to forego them.

Regardless of what some may say, Paul is an *apostle,* one directly *sent* by Jesus Christ. As an apostle he is free to claim all the privileges of such an office. Perhaps some may have argued that Paul was not a true apostle because he had not seen the Lord. But he says that he did see Jesus Christ. No doubt he mainly refers to his experience on the Damascus road, but on several further occa-

sions the Lord appeared to him as recorded in Acts. An
evidence of the fact that he is an apostle is the work he
has done in "planting" the Corinthian church. Even
though others may deny his authority, surely the Corinthians should not, for they have seen him work as an
apostle among them. They themselves are the "seal" of
his apostleship.

Evidently there are some who would "examine" him,
as if he were a criminal in a courtroom. His defense is
that he is a true apostle, that he does have the power to
eat and drink, to be married to a Christian woman, to
refrain from secular work and expect his support from
those to whom he ministers spiritually. It is obvious that
at the time Paul wrote these words he was either a bach-
elor, or a widower, and doubtless some of his opponents
criticized him as an ascetic, comparing him unfavorably
with Peter and the brethren of the Lord.

2. *The Proper Rewards of the Ministry* (9:7-14)

"Who goeth a warfare any time at his own charges?
who planteth a vineyard, and eateth not of the fruit
thereof? or who feedeth a flock, and eateth not of the
milk of the flock? Say I these things as a man? or saith
not the law the same also? For it is written in the law of
Moses, Thou shalt not muzzle the mouth of the ox that
treadeth out the corn. Doth God take care for oxen? Or
saith he it altogether for our sakes? For our sakes, no doubt,
this is written: that he that ploweth should plow in hope;
and that he that thresheth in hope should be partaker of
his hope. If we have sown unto you spiritual things, is it
a great thing if we shall reap your carnal things? If
others be partakers of this power over you, are not we

rather? Nevertheless we have not used this power; but suffer all things, lest we should hinder the gospel of Christ. Do ye not know that they which minister about holy things live of the things of the temple? and they which wait at the altar are partakers with the altar? Even so hath the Lord ordained that they which preach the gospel should live of the gospel."

Although Paul himself had not taken any money from the Corinthians, he defends his right and that of other Christian ministers to receive financial support from those to whom they minister. He compares the minister with a soldier, a vinedresser, a shepherd. Such are not expected to support themselves by some outside work. If any should say that these are just human illustrations, and that Paul is speaking "as a man" (that is, with mere human reasoning) he answers that the law of God teaches the same principle. Deuteronomy 25:4 is quoted, indicating that the ox which treaded out the grain was not to be muzzled. "The flail was not unknown but a common mode of threshing was to let the oxen tread the corn on the threshing floor" (*Pulpit Commentary*). In asking, "Doth God take care for oxen?" Paul does not mean to imply that the Lord cares nothing for animals, but rather that He cares much more for men. God spoke this precept about oxen *largely* for our sake, to show us that one who labors should receive his just reward. The one who plows and threshes "in hope" in spiritual things should be "partaker of his hope." In other words, the true Christian minister should be supported by the people to whom he ministers.

If one who sows in the material realm lives by the fruit of his labor, how much more should not one who sows "spiritual things" reap of the "carnal things" of those to whom he ministers. *Carnal* means *fleshly*. It is here used to refer to that which nourishes the flesh, or body. Since other teachers of various kinds are supported financially, how much more then should this be done for Christian teachers who spend their time giving out the Gospel of salvation and teaching the Word of God. Paul and his friends however did not in Corinth insist on using this authority of expecting their financial support from the people. Instead they were willing to "suffer all things," that is privation and hardship, rather than insist on their rights, because in this case they feared that such insistence would "hinder the gospel of Christ."

As another argument on this point, the apostle directs attention to the Levitical priests of the Old Testament. They ministered "about holy things," and received their living of these very things. The Book of Leviticus specifies that parts of the animals offered in sacrifice should go to the priests for their sustenance. The Lord Jesus Christ has ordained that this same principle should prevail in the present age (see Matt. 10:10; Luke 10:7).

3. *Paul's Curtailment of His Liberty "for the Gospel's Sake"* (9:15-23)

"But I have used none of these things: neither have I written these things, that it should be so done unto me: for it were better for me to die, than that any man should make my glorying void. For though I preach the gospel, I have nothing to glory of: for necessity is laid upon me; yea, woe is unto me, if I preach not the gospel! For if I do this thing willingly, I have a reward: but if against my will, a dispensation of the gospel is committed unto me. What is my reward then? Verily that, when I preach the gospel, I may make the gospel of Christ without charge, that I abuse not my power in the gospel. For though I be free from all men, yet have I made myself servant unto all, that I might gain the more. And unto the Jews I became as a Jew, that I might gain the Jews; to them that are under the law, as under the law, that I might gain them that are under the law; to them that are without law, as without law, (being not without law to God, but under the law to Christ,) that I might gain them that are without law. To the weak became I as weak, that I might gain the weak: I am made all things to all men, that I might by all means save some. And this I do for the gospel's sake, that I might be partaker thereof with you."

For the Gospel's sake, Paul has been willing to curtail his own liberty. He did not take financial remuneration from the Corinthians, neither does he now write simply to call it to their attention so that they might still provide for him. In fact, he would rather be dead than to have any man make "my glorying [or *boasting*] void." He boasted of the fact that the Gospel was free. He did not want to give any person grounds for saying that he (Paul) was teaching just for selfish purposes. And he well knew that some in Corinth would have said just that.

Lest he be misunderstood however he makes it plain that he has nothing to glory of in himself for preaching the Gospel. There is an inner compulsion upon him, similar to that Peter and John felt when they said: "For we cannot but speak the things which we have seen and heard" (Acts 4:20). His "woe is me" signifies that he would be utterly miserable if he did *not* preach the Gospel. So long as he performs his ministry "willingly"—without compulsion—then he receives a reward. But if there is a compulsion that forces him to do it, a stewardship of the Gospel is nevertheless committed to him, and he must some day account to God for it. The sole reward he desires is to be able to preach "the gospel of Christ without charge." He wants to win men to Christ, and to make it crystal-clear to all that salvation is entirely by grace. To claim a right that might in some particular instance hinder his message would actually be abusing his power in the Gospel.

Although Paul has been set truly free by the Lord Jesus, paradoxically he has deliberately made himself the "servant of all" so that by all means he may "gain the more" for Christ. In order to better accomplish his purpose he was ever willing to adapt himself to the people with whom he was dealing. To the Jews he became as a Jew; to the Gentiles, as one of them. Acts 13 and 14 provide excellent illustrations of this principle. Of course the apostle does not at all mean that he compromised the essentials of the Word of God, neither does he mean that he stooped to any evil deed. He does mean that whether dealing with men under the law (Jews) or "without law" (Gentiles) he adapted himself to their condition.

He hastens to explain that this does not signify that he is actually "without law to God," or in other words *lawless*. He is rather "under the law to Christ." "The expression is peculiar and might be literally rendered 'not lawless toward God, but inlawed to Christ.' . . . It is another way of saying, 'not under the law, but under (the rule of) grace' (Rom. 6:14)" (Scofield). Paul's chief aim in life was to win lost men to Christ, and for this purpose he became "all things to all men." Everything was done "for the gospel's sake" so that he might be partaker with other Christians of the joy of bringing souls to the Lord.

C. Running the Race—Self-discipline of the Christian (9:24-27)

"Know ye not that they which run in a race run all, but one receiveth the prize? So run, that ye may obtain. And every man that striveth for the mastery is temperate in all things. Now they do it to obtain a corruptible crown; but we an incorruptible. I therefore so run, not as uncertainly; so fight I, not as one that beateth the air: but I keep under my body, and bring it into subjection: lest that by any means, when I have preached to others, I myself should be a castaway."

Paul is still dealing with the subject of Christian liberty, and he here gives principles which are quite applicable to the original question concerning the eating of meat offered to idols. It is necessary for the true Christian to do more than merely abstain from manifestly evil things. If he is to "win the race" he must sternly discipline himself. "His reference is probably to the Isthmian games, named from the isthmus on which Corinth stood. These contests . . . constituted a great national and religious festival, and every second year drew eager throngs to the city of Corinth. Only freemen could contend in these games, and the contestants must give satisfactory proof that for ten months they had undergone the necessary preliminary training. For thirty days before the contests, all candidates were required to attend exercises at the gymnasium, and only when they had properly fulfilled all such conditions were they allowed to contend in the sight of the assembled throngs. The herald proclaimed the name and the country of each contestant, and also announced the name of the victor, who was crowned with a garland of pine leaves or parsley, or ivy. The family of the victor was regarded with honor, and when he returned to his native city a breach was made in the walls to allow him to enter, the purpose of this being to indicate that a town to which such a citizen belonged had no need of walls for its defense. The victorious hero was immortalized in verse; he was assigned a foremost seat when attending all future contests" (Erdman).

Paul argues that the true believer should view the Christian life in a similar manner, striving to win the prize. Two differences are however pointed out between the Christian race and an earthly contest. In the earthly contest, but one wins the prize; in the Christian life all can win. In the earthly contest, the prize is merely "a corruptible crown"; in the Christian life it is an incorruptible one.

But there are also *similarities*, things in the athlete which the Christian should imitate. The athlete is "temperate in all things." He abstains from all practices which might hinder his winning the race, even though these things may be harmless in themselves. The athlete has a definite purpose in mind, and he is always concentrating on that purpose. Therefore he mortifies the body and its natural desires. Paul likewise does the same, lest after he has been the means of starting others on this race, he himself might become "a castaway"—"disapproved"— that is, *disqualified*. This statement has nothing to do with his soul's salvation, regarding which he had perfect confidence (II Tim. 1:12). The thing he feared was that he might get into such a spiritual condition as to lose the reward he so much desired of the Lord Jesus Christ—to hear His voice say: "Well done, good and faithful servant."

D. Examples from Israel's History (10:1-13)

1. *The Privileges of the Israelites* (10:1-5)

"Moreover, brethren, I would not that ye should be ignorant, how that all our fathers were under the cloud, and all passed through the sea; and were all baptized unto Moses in the cloud and in the sea; and did all eat the same spiritual meat; and did all drink the same spiritual drink: for they drank of that spiritual Rock that followed them: and that Rock was Christ. But with many of them God was not well pleased: for they were overthrown in the wilderness."

Paul deals yet further with the general subject introduced by the question regarding meats offered to idols. He now proceeds to give real and graphic examples from the Old Testament history of Israel. These illustrations concern people of God who started well, but through self-indulgence and lack of self-discipline lost the reward.

The Israelites were led out of Egyptian bondage into liberty. The pillar of cloud guided them. The sea opened to deliver them. They were "baptized unto Moses," that is, they were brought into a deep personal relationship with Moses, and with all of the Mosaic economy for which he stood. They were provided with "spiritual meat"—the *manna.* They were provided with "spiritual drink"—from the *rock,* that represented Christ. An old Jewish legend claimed that the literal rock followed the Israelites through the wilderness. At least it is true that the "spiritual Rock" followed them. Christ Himself followed His people to supply all their *real* needs. But in spite of these great blessings and privileges which the people had, God was not pleased with "many of them." Sad to say only *two* in fact were pleasing to Him—Caleb and Joshua. The rest of the people became *castaways*— "overthrown in the wilderness."

2. *The Reasons for Their Becoming Castaways* (10:6-10)

"Now these things were our examples, to the intent that we should not lust after evil things, as they also lusted. Neither be ye idolaters, as were some of them; as it is written, The people sat down to eat and drink, and rose up to play. Neither let us commit fornication, as some of them committed, and fell in one day three and twenty thousand. Neither let us tempt Christ, as some of them also tempted, and were destroyed of serpents. Neither murmur ye, as some of them also murmured, and were destroyed of the destroyer."

Paul reminds us that all this is for "our examples." The people of Israel lusted for things the Lord had not provided. The full story can be read in Numbers 11:4 ff. They became enmeshed in acts of idolatry and sat down to an idol feast. This refers of course to their worship of the golden calf (Exod. 32:6). From this idol feast they arose to immoral festivity. They committed the sin of fornication—a sin very common in pagan worship, even in Corinth. Because of this many of the Israelites fell in a terrible judgment. They "tempted Christ" by murmuring and complaining. Finally there was open defiance which was punished by a plague of fiery serpents (see Num. 21:6). They murmured against their God-appointed leaders (Num. 16:41-49). For this they felt the wrath of "the destroyer," that is, the destroying angel.

3. *The Spiritual Application for the Present Day* (10:11-13)

"Now all these things happened unto them for ensamples: and they are written for our admonition, upon whom the ends of the world are come. Wherefore let him that thinketh he standeth take heed lest he fall. There hath no temptation taken you but such as is common to man: but God is faithful, who will not suffer you to be tempted above that ye are able; but will with the temptation also make a way to escape, that ye may be able to bear it."

In words of great significance the apostle advises us that all these things which happened to the Old Testament Israelites have a spiritual message for modern men. They are *examples* (or *types*). They were recorded in the Bible not simply to give us interesting historical information, but to *admonish* us, living as we do in such a favored position at the "ends of the ages." One who is depending on being outwardly numbered among the people of God and therefore "thinketh he standeth" is warned to take heed lest he fall, as did those Israelites of old.

In a most gracious conclusion to the section the apostle reminds us, however, that no temptation (or *test*) has befallen us but such as is common to humanity. It is definitely promised that God will not allow us to be swept away by an overpowering temptation. He will not permit us to experience anything beyond that which we can bear. With each temptation He will mercifully provide some way in which we can secure the victory over it.

E. Christian Liberty and the Lord's Table (10:14-33)

"Wherefore, my dearly beloved, flee from idolatry. I speak as to wise men; judge ye what I say. The cup of blessing which we bless, is it not the communion of the blood of Christ? The bread which we break, is it not the communion of the body of Christ? For we being many are one bread, and one body: for we are all partakers of that one bread. Behold Israel after the flesh: are not they which eat of the sacrifices partakers of the altar? What say I then? that the idol is anything, or that which is offered in sacrifice to idols is anything? But I say, that the things which the Gentiles sacrifice, they sacrifice to devils, and not to God: and I would not that ye should have fellowship with devils. Ye cannot drink the cup of the Lord, and the cup of devils: ye cannot be partakers of the Lord's table, and of the table of devils. Do we provoke the Lord to jealousy? are we stronger than he? All things are lawful for me, but all things are not expedient: all things are lawful for me, but all things edify not. Let no man seek his own, but every man another's wealth. Whatsoever is sold in the shambles, that eat, asking no question for conscience sake. For the earth is the Lord's and the fullness thereof. If any of them that believe not bid you to a feast, and ye be disposed to go; whatsoever is set before you, eat, asking no question for conscience sake. But if any man say unto you, This is offered in sacrifice unto idols, eat not for his sake that shewed it, and for conscience sake: for the earth is the Lord's, and the fullness thereof: conscience, I say, not thine own, but of the other: for why is my liberty judged of another man's conscience? For if I by grace be a partaker, why am I evil spoken of for that for which I give thanks?

Whether therefore ye eat, or drink, or whatsoever ye do, do all to the glory of God. Give none offense, neither to the Jews, nor to the Gentiles, nor to the church of God: even as I please all men in all things, not seeking mine own profit, but the profit of many, that they may be saved."

There is now a return to the subject with which this entire section of the epistle began—the eating of meat offered to idols. A further and final word on the whole matter is given. While the actual eating of such meat may be in the realm of doubtful things, we can know with absolute certainty that anything which is really idolatry is wrong. From idolatry we should "flee." In such matters it is best not to see how near to sin we can get without being contaminated, but rather how far we can stay away from it. When Paul says: "I speak to wise men; judge ye what I say" (v. 15), he may possibly be using irony as in certain earlier verses. This may however be taken as a simple acknowledgment that as Christians they do have true wisdom.

For a purpose, the apostle alludes to the outstanding ceremony of Christian worship—the Lord's Supper. In this sacrament, the cup is "the communion of the blood of Christ." The word rendered here as *communion* is in 1:9 translated *fellowship.* The bread is our *fellowship* in the Body of Christ. By partaking of these symbolic elements we proclaim that we are saved by the redeeming blood of Christ and have now become members of His Body. So, although saved people are many separate individuals, nevertheless they become in Christ "one loaf—one Body." It is unthinkable that those who have fellowship with Christ, and are members of His Body should also have fellowship with demons.

In the case of Old Testament Israel, the priests and people who partook of the sacrifices aligned themselves with all that the altar stood for. Can Paul, who has previously said that an idol is "nothing in the world," now be implying that an idol is something after all? No, but nevertheless behind the idol worship there does exist demon power. So then those who worship idols are not merely worshiping that which is nonexistent but are really worshiping demons. The apostle does not want a believer to do anything whereby he would be aligning himself with demons. Christianity is of necessity an "exclusive religion" because no person can worship both God and demons. Our God is a "jealous God" (Exod. 20:5). If those who are His servants should take part in idolatrous worship His anger would indeed be aroused. And, Paul asks, can we afford to arouse His anger? To incur His displeasure? "Are we stronger than he?"

Again a principle of similar nature to that in 6:12 is enunciated: "All things are lawful for me, but all things are not expedient: all things are lawful for me, but all things edify not." We must not judge our actions simply by the standard of what is *lawful*. We must consider whether an action is "expedient," that is, does it bring profit. We must determine whether it "edifies"—builds up spiritually. So the Christian must not test a doubtful thing solely by whether it is *lawful,* but must also decide whether it is *profitable* and *edifying*. He must not consider merely his own personal interest, but must be concerned as to what effect his life will have on others.

At last Paul is ready to give a direct answer to the Corinthians' problem. The reference in verse 25 to "shambles" means a "meat market." A Christian can buy meat at such a place without making special inquiry regarding each piece. He receives it as a provision from the Lord who owns "the cattle upon a thousand hills" (Ps. 50:10). In like manner a Christian who is invited to dine at the home of an unsaved friend is free to accept if he so wishes, and does not need to make special inquiry about each portion of food he is offered. But it is expressly stipulated that if at such a place someone specifically informs him that the meat has been used in idol worship, then the Christian should refuse to eat it, for the sake of the one who showed it, the latter being evidently troubled about the matter. This should be done lest the conscience of the informer be damaged and defiled.

In the close of verses 29 and 30 Paul either quotes from the inquiry addressed to him by the Corinthians, or else puts himself in the place of the strong Christian who feels he can conscientiously eat the meat and asks why he should be judged by another's conscience. Verses 31-33 give the answer to these inquiries. It is because the true Christian should want everything he does to be done to the glory of God. He should be anxious not to "give offense," which means to put a "stumbling block" before another person, whether that person be a Jew, a Gentile, or a Christian. In accordance with this principle, Paul does not live to please himself, or to seek merely his own selfish profit. He lives to please others, to bring profit to others, and by this he means—to lead others to Christ.

F. Instructions Regarding Modesty in Women (11:1-16)

"Be ye followers of me, even as I also am of Christ. Now I praise you, brethren, that ye remember me in all things, and keep the ordinances, as I delivered them to you. But I would have you know, that the head of every man is Christ; and the head of the woman is the man; and the head of Christ is God. Every man praying or prophesying, having his head covered, dishonoreth his head. But every woman that prayeth or prophesieth with her head uncovered dishonoreth her head: for that is even all one as if she were shaven. For if the woman be not covered, let her also be shorn: but if it be a shame for a woman to be shorn or shaven, let her be covered. For a man indeed ought not to cover his head, forasmuch as he is the image and glory of God: but the woman is the glory of the man. For the man is not of the woman; but the woman of the man. Neither was the man created for the woman; but the woman for the man. For this cause ought the woman to have power on her head because of the angels. Nevertheless neither is the man without the woman, neither the woman without the man, in the Lord. For as the woman is of the man, even so is the man also by the woman; but all things of God. Judge in yourselves: is it comely that a woman pray unto God uncovered? Doth not even nature itself teach you, that, if a man have long hair, it is a shame unto him? But if a woman have long hair, it is a glory to her: for her hair is given her for a covering. But if any man seem to be contentious, we have no such custom, neither the churches of God."

Some people deem Paul to be a veritable enemy of womanhood. This judgment is largely based on his writings in I Corinthians 7 and in the present chapter. He should more properly be considered as the *emancipator*. At a time when women were generally regarded as far inferior to men, and little better than slaves (and in heathen lands this is more or less true even today), the apostle taught something quite different. (See, for example, Gal. 3:28.)

In Corinth it seems that certain Christian women had been so swept off their feet by their new-found liberty in Christ that they were discarding the established customs of modesty of that day. Thus they were bringing reproach on the name of Christ and on His work. Here again is another matter that can be at least roughly classified under the heading of an abuse of Christian liberty.

This problem, like that regarding meat offered to idols, reflects a custom which is no longer in existence in this modern day, at least in the western world. To benefit from the teaching we must therefore separate that which is purely local in nature from the basic underlying principles. In first century Corinth, decent women usually wore veils when going around in public where men were present. "Loose women in those days went bareheaded, and were found in the streets unblushingly seeking those who might be companions with them in their sin and wickedness. Women who sought to live in chastity and purity were very particular never to appear in public unveiled. The unveiled woman was the careless woman, the immoral woman; the veiled woman was the careful wife or mother who was concerned about her character and her reputation" (Ironside).

The opening verse of chapter 11 can be more properly considered as concluding the thought of chapter 10. Paul calls upon Christians to imitate him, in connection with his principle of life as found in 10:33, even as he did Christ. With the commendation of 11:2, the new discussion commences. First there is a word of praise for the Corinthians because they are generally observing the "ordinances"—the apostolic teachings on these various subjects being discussed. But regarding a particular matter, Paul must criticize. This criticism he introduces by stating a general principle with regard to *subordination*. Every man is subordinate to Christ, and should therefore be submissive to Him: Christ is his leader. The woman is to follow the leadership of the man. This directly has in view the marriage relationship of husband and wife, though there may be a general application outside that realm. The "head of Christ is God." Though equal with the Father, the Son has voluntarily become submissive to Him. He does the Father's will. He says, "My Father is greater than I" (John 14:28). "In the same way that the divine Son is dependent upon the Father and subject to Him, so is a husband subordinate to Christ, and so, too is a wife subordinate to her husband. The principle involves no humiliation, no injustice, no wrong. It recognizes a difference of function and responsibility, but it precludes selfishness, harshness, and unkindness. If the husband remembers his relation to Christ, he will not abuse his relation to the wife he is expected to honor and support and protect and love" (Erdman).

In public worship, the man should pray or prophesy with his head uncovered. Otherwise he dishonors his Head (that is, Christ). The woman on the contrary should wear a veil. It must be said again that this statement reflects local conditions in Corinth where the woman who went around publicly with unveiled face, and with shorn or shaven hair, was a prostitute. Because of this, if the Christian woman discards her veil, she casts a reflection on and dishonors her "head" (that is, her husband). By the way, it must be noted here that the apostle clearly implies that if a woman is called to do so, and if she fulfills the necessary conditions of decorum, it is proper for her publicly to *pray* (which is speaking to God about men) and to *prophesy* (which is speaking to men about God). Acts 2:17 further verifies this teaching. It may be justly added that there are several verses in other books which when superficially considered may seem to contradict this teaching. These other verses will however be found to have their proper interpretation in their own context, without involving any conflict whatever with the present passage.

In decided contrast to synagogue usage, Paul states that the man ought not in public worship to cover his head. He is "the image and glory of God." All were made in God's image. Only Christ fully realized the ideal of always glorifying the Father in His humanity. But man is to reflect the glory of God.

The woman should be "the glory of man." "The woman is created in the *image of God* as well as the man (Gen. 1:26, 27). But as the moon in relation to the sun (Gen. 37:9) so woman shines not so much with light direct from God as with light derived from man—i.e., in her order *in creation*—though *in grace* she comes into *direct* communication with God" (Fausset).

When Paul says: "For the man is not of the woman; but the woman of the man. Neither was the man created for the woman; but the woman for the man" he directly refers to Genesis 2:18-22—"And the Lord God said, It is not good that the man should be alone; I will make him a help meet for him. And out of the ground the Lord God formed every beast of the field, and every fowl of the air; and brought them unto Adam to see what he would call them: and whatsoever Adam called every living creature, that was the name thereof. And Adam gave names to all cattle, and to the fowl of the air, and to every beast of the field; but for Adam there was not found a help meet for him. And the Lord God caused a deep sleep to fall upon Adam, and he slept: and he took one of his ribs, and closed up the flesh instead thereof; and the rib, which the Lord God had taken from man, made he a woman, and brought her unto the man."

The statement of verse 10: "For this cause ought the woman to have power on her head because of the angels," is somewhat mysterious. In the American Standard Version the word *power* is changed to "a sign of authority." The probable meaning seems to be that angels are unseen observers of our religious services, and they are offended when things are not done "decently and in order."

A word of caution is added lest either sex think that it is complete or independent in itself. The man is not complete "without the woman," neither is the woman complete "without the man." "They were made to be a mutual comfort and blessing, not one a slave and the other a tyrant" (Matthew Henry). The woman is "of the man" in the sense of being made from the rib of Adam. At the same time "the man is also by the woman" in natural birth (cf. Job 14:1).

An additional appeal is made to "nature": "Doth not even nature itself teach you?" (v. 14). The apostle evidently uses the word *nature* here in the sense of *instinct*. Is it not generally thought among people everywhere that if a man wears his hair very long it is a reproach, but that on the other hand if a woman's hair is very long it is a glory to her? "If it should not be taken away from her, no more should the veil of which her hair is the natural symbol" (Erdman). H. A. Ironside happily remarks: "In the presence of God she covers her chief beauty in order that no mind may be turned from Christ to her beautiful hair."

The expression "we have no such custom, neither the churches of God," has sometimes been applied to the first part of verse 16. It seems better however to apply it to the subject of the entire section: women removing their veils while praying or prophesying.

It is interesting to note that because of this passage it is still customary in many places for women to wear hats at formal services of worship. This illustrates the fact that it is always easier to get people to follow customs than to understand principles of action. As to applying the general teaching to ourselves, it can certainly be done in this way: on things not in themselves right or wrong, it is proper to follow local customs as to modest behavior, lest in any way we cast a "stumbling block" before another.

G. Instructions Regarding the Lord's Supper (11:17-34)

"Now in this that I declare unto you I praise you not, that ye come together not for the better, but for the worse. For first of all, when ye come together in the church, I hear that there be divisions among you; and I partly believe it. For there must be also heresies among you, that they which are approved may be made manifest among you. When ye come together therefore into one place, this is not to eat the Lord's supper. For in eating every one taketh before other his own supper: and one is hungry, and another is drunken. What? have ye not houses to eat and to drink in? or despise ye the church of God, and shame them that have not? What shall I say to you? shall I praise you in this? I praise you not. For I have received of the Lord that which also I delivered unto you, That the Lord Jesus the same night in which he was betrayed took bread: and when he had given thanks, he brake it, and said, Take, eat: this is my body, which is broken for you: this do in remembrance of me. After the same manner also he took the cup, when he had supped, saying, This cup is the new testament in my blood: this do ye, as oft as ye drink it, in remembrance of me. For as often as ye eat this bread, and drink this cup, ye do shew the Lord's death till he come. Wherefore whosoever shall eat this bread, and drink this cup of the Lord, unworthily, shall be guilty of the body and blood of the Lord. But let a man examine himself, and so let him eat of that bread, and drink of that cup. For he that eateth and drinketh unworthily, eateth and drinketh damnation to himself, not discerning the Lord's body. For this cause many are weak and sickly among you, and many sleep. For if we would judge ourselves, we should not be judged. But when we are judged, we are chastened of the Lord, that we should not be condemned with the world. Wherefore, my brethren, when ye come together to eat, tarry one for another. And if any man hunger, let him eat at home; that ye come not together unto condemnation. And the rest will I set in order when I come."

In this next matter of which the apostle is forced to speak, he affirms that he can find nothing to praise in the Corinthians' conduct. When they meet together, instead of the service resulting in spiritual blessing, the fact is that they are worse off afterward than they were before. Why? Because they are carrying over their spirit of divisions even into the worship and fellowship services of the church. Paul hesitates to believe that conditions are as bad as he has heard, but he "partly believes it." They seem to think that they must have "heresies" (or, better, *schisms,* or *factions* as in the A.S.V.) among them, so that those who are so highly valuing human wisdom may feel superior to the others.

This present section obviously reflects something which commentators tell us was a common practice in the early Church. The Christians would often meet together for a fellowship meal (called a "love feast") which was followed by the celebration of the Lord's Supper. It was customary at such feasts for those who were wealthy to bring much and for those who were poor to bring their little, each then sharing alike. But at Corinth, sad to say, in their "love feasts" some were getting a lot to eat and others nothing. Some were even getting intoxicated. Paul sharply rebukes such conduct. He insists that if their main purpose is to satisfy their appetites, then they should stay at home and eat there. By this disgraceful conduct they were despising the "church of God," that is, their fellow Christians. The rich were shaming those who were so poor that they could bring little. The apostle repeats his assertion that he can find nothing at all to praise in such conduct.

Paul then seeks to correct the false attitude by the true doctrine, by a reminder as to the sacredness of the Lord's Supper. Verses 23-26 are too familiar to need extended exposition. It should be observed that the apostle claims to have received this teaching by direct inspiration from the Lord. He also states that he had previously told this to the Corinthians: "I deliver*ed* unto you." But obviously they were neglecting this truth which they knew. The Lord's Supper is said here to be a symbolic memorial which looks in two directions—backward to the atoning death of Christ, and forward to His second coming.

The warning, "whosoever shall eat this bread, and drink this cup of the Lord, unworthily, shall be guilty of the body and blood of the Lord," is too often lifted bodily from its original context and made to bear an entirely different sense from that which was intended. *Unworthily* does not at all refer to the *character* of the communicant, but to his *conduct* at the communion service. The American Standard Version renders it "in an unworthy manner." The rebuke is aimed at unruly conduct like that described in verses 20-22. So the statement does *not* command true believers to abstain from the Lord's Supper merely because they feel unworthy in themselves. Neither does it countenance a Christian in thinking he can continue in known sin with impunity, if he simply refrains from partaking of the communion elements. *Damnation* in verse 29 is, according to its present usage, too strong a word—better is the word *judgment* as in the American Standard Version. The same Greek word is in James 3:1 translated "condemnation." A person guilty of such disorders around the Lord's Table brings upon himself *condemnation.*

Paul explicitly states that because of such sins, certain Christians at Corinth had already suffered bodily affliction, and some had died. Not *all* physical affliction is punishment for sin, but evidently *some* is. Since further details of the particular cases the apostle had in mind are unknown, it is useless to speculate on the subject.

It is affirmed as a general principle that if we would practice self-judgment, then we would escape such chastening of the Lord. If we are quick to detect and confess sin when it appears in our lives, we will avoid much trouble. When we fail to do this, the Lord has to chasten us for our own good, to draw us to repentance so that He will not have to condemn us with the unbelieving world.

For the Corinthians' particular problem a final practical word is offered: at their love feasts, they are not to selfishly push ahead of others, but rather to courteously "tarry one for another." If it happens that a man is so hungry that he feels unable to do this, then he should "eat at home." "The rest"—further questions about the Lord's Supper—Paul promises to "set in order" when he makes a future visit to Corinth.

Chapter Seven

ERRORS CORRECTED:
CONCERNING SPIRITUAL GIFTS
(12—14)

A. Spiritual Gifts Sovereignly Controlled by the
Holy Spirit (12:1-11)

Now concerning spiritual gifts, brethren, I would not have you ignorant. Ye know that ye were Gentiles, carried away unto these dumb idols, even as ye were led. Wherefore I give you to understand, that no man speaking by the Spirit of God calleth Jesus accursed: and that no man can say that Jesus is the Lord, but by the Holy Ghost. Now there are diversities of gifts, but the same Spirit. And there are differences of administrations, but same Lord. And there are diversities of operations, but it is the same God which worketh all in all. But the manifestation of the Spirit is given to every man to profit withal. For to one is given by the Spirit the word of wisdom; to another the word of knowledge by the same Spirit; to another faith by the same Spirit; to another the gifts of healing by the same Spirit; to another the working of miracles; to another prophecy; to another discerning of spirits; to another divers kinds of tongues; to another the interpretation of tongues: but all these worketh that one and the selfsame Spirit, dividing to every man severally as he will."

Paul now turns to "spiritual things," matters relating to the Holy Spirit. He earnestly desires for Christians to be familiar with these vitally important truths. The Corinthians are reminded that they were once unsaved Gentiles, serving "dumb idols." But now, the Holy Spirit having dealt with their hearts, they call Jesus "Lord." Surely this is indeed the central fact of "spiritual things"—the greatest work of the Holy Spirit is to reveal Jesus to us as the Lord (John 16:14). If any person rejects and reviles Jesus such a one cannot possibly be speaking by the Spirit of God. When Paul says that "no man can say that Jesus is the Lord, but by the Holy Ghost," he does not of course mean that a person could not hypocritically call Jesus "Lord." For an example of this see Matthew 7:21-23. He does mean that the one who truly knows Jesus as his Lord has listened to the voice of the Holy Spirit.

In speaking directly of spiritual gifts, the apostle is talking about capacities or abilities for service given by the Holy Spirit to individual Christians. There are diversities (or *distinctions*) in such gifts, but only one Holy Spirit who bestows them. There are also different ways in which these gifts are used—"differences of administration." Different people even use in a diverse way similar gifts. Nevertheless but one Lord directs it all. There are differences of "operation"—manifestation of the divine energy—but only one God who works "all in all." All these various manifestations are given "to every man" for the general good of the whole church ("to profit withal").

Nine particular gifts of the Holy Spirit are listed. The list is not intended to be exhaustive. A similar list in verse 28 contains several items not found here. It should also be noted that included in this list are gifts we think of as "ordinary," as well as others we usually term "miraculous." As to whether these so-called "miraculous gifts" still continue down to the present day, reverent scholars disagree. In this connection Dr. A. R. Fausset's cogent words are worthy of careful thought: "The ordinary and permanent gifts are comprehended with the extraordinary without distinction, as both alike flow from the indwelling Spirit of life. The extraordinary gift, so far from making professors more peculiarly *saints* than in our day, did not always even prove that such persons were saved at all (Matt. 7:22). They were needed at first: (1) as a pledge to Christians who had just passed over from Judaism or heathendom, that God was in the Church; (2) for the propagation of Christianity in the Church; (3) for edifying the Church. They continued down to the third century, when the Church rose on the decline of heathenism. They were rare after the apostolic age. Now that we have the *whole written* New Testament, which they had not, and Christianity established by miracles, we need no further miracle to attest the truth. So the pillar of cloud which guided the Israelites was withdrawn when they were sufficiently assured of the Divine presence, the manifestation of God's glory being thence-forward enclosed in the Most Holy place."

What about Christ's promise in John 14:12?—"Verily, verily, I say unto you, He that believeth on me, the works that I do shall he do also; and greater works than these shall he do; because I go unto my Father." "I cannot doubt that this promise refers to the miraculous gifts which the first generation of Christians had the power to exercise, as we read everywhere in the Acts of the Apostles. That the sick were healed, the dead raised, and devils cast out by the disciples after the Lord ascended, is quite plain and this fulfilled the words now before us. I can see no reason to suppose that our Lord meant the promise to be fulfilled after the generation He left on earth was dead. We have no right to expect miracles now. If miracles were continually in the Church, they would cease to be miracles. We never see them in the Bible except at some great crisis in the Church's history, such as the deliverance of Israel from Egypt. The Irvingite theory, that the Church would always have miraculous gifts, if men only had faith, seems to me a violent straining of the text" (Ryle).

In the dispensing of spiritual gifts, one person is given the ability (after due study) of getting a thorough grasp of divine teaching—"the word of knowledge." Another is gifted in being able to apply what he knows in a wise way—"the word of wisdom." Some receive the gift of "faith." The reference here is not to *saving faith* for all of those referred to in this passage are saved, but rather to faith for some unusual project or work for the Lord. A good example of this would be George Müller of Bristol, "the orphans' friend." Some believers (though not all) were given gifts of "healings," while some wrought other kinds of miracles or prophesied. Why do none today apparently have these miraculous gifts? Is not the answer to be found in the words of verse 11? "But all these worketh that one and the selfsame Spirit, dividing to every man severally as he will."

Some Christians are quite gifted in "discerning spirits," in judging whether they are good or bad (cf. I John 4:1). Others (but *not* all) are given the gift of speaking in "tongues." Opinions differ as to whether the reference here is to speaking in languages not previously learned as the apostles did in Acts 2, or to some sort of ecstatic speaking in a mysterious language not of man at all. Another person is given a gift, says the apostle, of translating such speaking in tongues. In all the true gifts, the Holy Spirit works, distributing them according to His own sovereign will.

B. The Body of Christ Compared with the Human Body (12:12-31)

"For as the body is one, and hath many members, and all the members of that one body, being many, are one body: so also is Christ. For by one Spirit are we all baptized into one body, whether we be Jews or Gentiles, whether we be bond or free; and have been all made to drink into one Spirit. For the body is not one member, but many. If the foot shall say, Because I am not the hand, I am not of the body; is it therefore not of the body? And if the ear shall say, Because I am not the eye, I am not of the body; is it therefore not of the body? If the whole body were an eye, where were the hearing? If the whole were hearing, where were the smelling? But now hath God set the members every one of them in the body, as it hath pleased him. And if they were all one member, where were the body? But now are they many members, yet but one body. And the eye cannot say unto the hand, I have no need of thee: nor again the head to the feet, I have no need of you. Nay, much more those members of the body, which seem to be more feeble, are necessary: and those members of the body, which we think to be less honorable, upon these we bestow more abundant honor; and our uncomely parts have more abundant comeliness. For our comely parts have no need: but God hath tempered the body together, having given more abundant honor to that part which lacked: That there should be no schism in the body; but that the members should have the same care one for another. And whether one member suffer, all the members suffer with it; or one member be honored, all the members rejoice with it. Now ye are the body of Christ, and members in particular. And God hath set some in the church, first apostles, secondarily prophets, thirdly teachers, after that miracles, then gifts of healings, helps, governments, diversities of tongues. Are all apostles? are all prophets? are all teachers? are all workers of miracles? Have all the gifts of healing? do all speak with tongues? do all interpret? But covet earnestly the best gifts: and yet show I unto you a more excellent way."

To illustrate the fact that different believers although guided by the same Spirit, have different gifts, Paul now turns to a beautiful figure of the interrelationship between Christ and all of His own. The picture is that of the Church as the spiritual Body of Christ, and it is a familiar one to readers of the New Testament (cf. Rom. 12:4, 5; Col. 1:18; Eph. 1:22, 23; 4:1-16).

Although it has many members with diverse functions and duties, the human body is nevertheless one organism. A single life flows through it all. The "body of Christ" is the same—many members but just one Body. Every true Christian has been baptized into that one Body by the agency of the Holy Spirit. All believers have been made to "drink of one Spirit." This is truly "living water" (see John 4:10; 7:37-39; Acts 10:45).

In an almost humorous way, the apostle applies this figure to the particular situation which existed in the church at Corinth. Those possessing the more spectacular gifts were evidently proud, considering themselves better than others. Those possessing less spectacular gifts were on the contrary inclined to be disgruntled and so to waste the talent they had. Paul shows graphically the foolishness of such an attitude. The foot and the ear do not say that because they are not the hand or the eye they are not in the human body. God sets each as it pleases Him and each serves well in its place.

Those parts of the body which seem more important still have no right to say that they do not need those which seem less necessary. Parts which are more *"feeble"* (that is, more *delicate,* such as the brain) are quite essential. On members which we consider "less honorable" and even "uncomely" (like the belly and feet) we bestow "more abundant honor," covering them with clothes or shoes. God Himself has "tempered the body together," giving to each part its necessary function, so that those we may think of as less attractive nevertheless have very important duties to perform. In it all, each member is to do its own work in its own place, each helping any other when need requires. When one member suffers, all suffer. Any person who has had a toothache or a backache can testify to the truth of this assertion! If one member is honored, as when the wreath is placed on the victor's *head,* "all the members rejoice with it." The spiritual application of all this is so self-evident as not to require direct statement.

Each Christian belongs to the spiritual Body of Christ, and each has a particular service to perform as a member of that Body. Surely then one member should not be jealous of another, neither should one look with scorn upon others. It is interesting to observe that verse 28 lists certain gifts in their relative importance. First are *apostles*. Then come *prophets*. The word is probably used here in its typical New Testament sense (see 14:3), referring to what we nowadays would call *preachers*. Other items in the list need no explanation except for "helps" which refers to the special ability to help others, and "governments"—gifts of leadership and administration.

Obviously no one gift is given to *all* Christians, any more than all the human body could possess the gift of seeing (v. 17). Some gifts are better than others, in that they help the possessor to be of greater service. It is proper to earnestly desire such gifts, for since the Holy Spirit bestows them in a sovereign way, it is evident that He can confer them on whomsoever He wishes. Yet as important as these things are, Paul promises to show "a more excellent way" than that of mere gifts. This way is the *way of love* to which the apostle devotes the next chapter in its entirety. Unless gifts are used in a spirit of love, they are of little value. Love is the most important thing of all!

C. The More Excellent Way—That of Love (13)

This is one of the most noted and best loved chapters in the entire Bible. Christ often taught the importance of love (see, for example, Mark 12:28-34; John 15:12 and similar passages). In the present chapter Paul uses the same Greek word (improperly translated in the A.V. by the word *charity*). "Charity is love to God, creating in us love towards our neighbor" (Fausset). This chapter (I Cor. 13) clearly affirms that a real spirit of love for God and for our fellow men is absolutely essential, and without it everything else is valueless.

1. *The Supreme Importance of Love* (13:1-3)

"Though I speak with the tongues of men and of angels, and have not love, I am become as sounding brass, or a tinkling cymbal. And though I have the gift of prophecy, and understand all mysteries, and all knowledge; and though I have all faith, so that I could remove mountains, and have not love, I am nothing. And though I bestow all my goods to feed the poor, and though I give my body to be burned, and have not love, it profiteth me nothing."

Without love, even the greatest powers of eloquence and speech are worthless. Even though one had like Balaam the gift of prophecy, though he understood the deep things of God, possessed a thorough knowledge of the Word, had sufficient faith to perform mighty miracles, and yet was devoid of love, he would be simply a cipher.

If a person was self-sacrificing in his liberality to the poor, and was courageous enough even to "give his body to be burned," as did the three young friends of Daniel, yet had no love, his acts would not really profit him anything.

2. *The Characteristics of Love* (13:4-7)

"Love suffereth long, and is kind; love envieth not; love vaunteth not itself, is not puffed up, doth not behave itself unseemly, seeketh not her own, is not easily provoked, thinketh no evil; rejoiceth not in iniquity, but rejoiceth in the truth; beareth all things, believeth all things, hopeth all things, endureth all things."

Love is described as patient, not jealous, not proud and boastful. Love is courteous, unselfish, good-natured, is not suspicious. Love does not rejoice in wickedness, but rather rejoices when truth and purity prevail. Love uncomplainingly endures, looks on "the bright side," is hopeful, and patient in persecution.

3. *The Abiding Nature of Love* (13:8-13)

"Love never faileth: but whether there be prophecies, they shall fail; whether there be tongues, they shall cease; whether there be knowledge it shall vanish away. For we know in part, and we prophesy in part. But when that which is perfect is come, then that which is in part shall be done away. When I was a child, I spake as a child, I understood as a child, I thought as a child: but when I became a man, I put away childish things. For now we see through a glass, darkly; but then face to face: now I know in part; but then shall I know even as also I am known. And now abideth faith, hope, love, these three; but the greatest of these is love."

Love never *fails*. The Greek word here translated "fail" means to fall to the ground like the petals off a flower. On the contrast prophecy, tongues, spiritual knowledge will finally "be done away" when the Lord returns in the fullness of His glory. Now our knowledge of these matters is partial. The prophecies we have are also partial (cf. Heb. 1:1). But when we know and understand fully, when we see the Lord face to face, the partial knowledge we possess at present will be of no further concern. The present state of things, even with the very real knowledge granted by God to believers, is to be compared with the future perfect state like the knowledge of a child compares with that of a mature adult. In Paul's day, mirrors of brass were used. At best these were not so bright and distinct as our modern glass mirrors. Our present knowledge is said to be like the image seen indistinctly in one of those brass mirrors. Our future knowledge will be direct and

full—"face to face." Then we shall fully know, even as
God fully knows us now. It should be remembered however that although our present knowledge is partial, it is
nevertheless real—"*I know* in part."

The gifts which the Corinthians prized so highly—
prophecy, tongues, religious knowledge—are transitory.
Love, which abides, is far superior. It is even said by the
apostle to be greater than two other abiding things—
faith and hope. Just why this is so he does not directly
state. Four possible reasons are aptly suggested by the
Pulpit Commentary. Love is greater than faith and hope
(1) because it is the root of the other two; (2) it is for
others, while faith and hope are largely for ourselves; (3)
faith and hope are human but God is love; (4) faith and
hope can only work by love, and show themselves by
love.

D. The Greatest Gift—That of Prophecy (14)

From the various gifts mentioned in chapter 12, the
apostle selects three for discussion in the present chapter.
These are: (1) prophecy, (2) speaking in tongues, (3) interpretation of tongues. Certain rules are provided for
the use of these gifts, and their comparative importance
is evaluated. The Corinthians were evidently quite proud
of their gift of tongues. Paul shows that this gift is much
less important than others, and that it is not to be used
in public at all, unless certain requirements are met. As
some in our day claim to possess this gift, this chapter is
especially interesting, being the outstanding passage in
the entire Bible on the subject of tongues. "The gift of
tongues is coveted and even claimed by many members

of the modern Church. Whether this claim is true or false is a question of fact to be established upon evidence. Most persons are convinced that sufficient evidence to support the claim has never been produced. They believe the alleged experience to be a form of hysteria or self-deception or delusion. In any event, it is well to remember that Paul regarded tongues as the least to be desired of all the gifts of the Spirit, and found it necessary to warn the Corinthian Christians against the abuse and improper estimate of this gift" (Erdman).

First, all Christians are urged to pursue the way of love just discussed in chapter 13. "Follow after love, and desire spiritual gifts, but rather that ye may prophesy" (14:1). If love is given first place then it is proper to be ambitious for spiritual gifts so that one may be of more service in the Body of Christ. *Prophecy* is singled out as the best gift of all.

"For he that speaketh in an unknown tongue speaketh not unto men, but unto God: for no man understandeth him; howbeit in the spirit he speaketh mysteries" (14:2). The word *unknown* in this verse (and those that follow) is in italics, meaning that it is not to be found in the original Greek text of the New Testament. So Paul refers here to one who is able to "speak in a tongue." Other references in the historical books to this gift are to be found only in Mark 16:17; Acts 2; Acts 10; Acts 19. On the day of Pentecost the disciples spoke not in "unknown" tongues, but in living languages. On that particular occasion men were present who understood these various languages, and bore testimony to this fact (Acts 2:7-11). However on other occasions there was no one present who understood the actual languages used. This speaking in tongues was not a giving out of the Gospel, but rather a bursting forth in praise of God (cf. Acts 2:11), which other persons around would not ordinarily be able to understand. But on the contrary, the one who prophesies (or "forthtells" the Word of God) by edifying, exhorting, and comforting brings blessing to all those who hear him. "But he that prophesieth speaketh unto men to edification, and exhortation, and comfort" (14:3).

"He that speaketh in an unknown tongue edifieth himself; but he that prophesieth edifieth the church" (14:4). It is evident that the one who really spoke "in a tongue" found blessing in the experience, and was personally edified. But the one who proclaims God's Word in plain language accomplishes something greater—he edifies *others,* the church. "I would that ye all spake with tongues, but rather that ye prophesied: for greater is he that prophesieth than he that speaketh with tongues, except he interpret, that the church may receive edifying" (14:5). These words make it plain that not all in Corinth were able to speak in tongues. Paul indicates that if all did he would be glad, but that he would much rather that all could prophesy. The one who prophesies is greater than he that speaks in tongues, unless the latter can interpret into understandable language that which he speaks. Then others may know what was said and receive a blessing from it.

"Now, brethren, if I come unto you speaking with tongues, what shall I profit you, except I shall speak to you either by revelation, or by knowledge, or by prophesying, or by doctrine?" (14:6). Even the apostle Paul himself would not bring blessing when he came to Corinth if he spoke in tongues that no one could understand. He is only able to edify people when he brings to them *revelation* from God, *knowledge* of spiritual truth, *prophesy-*

ing like that of verse 3, or *doctrine,* by which he means simple teaching.

"And even things without life giving sound, whether pipe or harp, except they give a distinction in the sounds, how shall it be known what is piped or harped? For if the trumpet give an uncertain sound, who shall prepare himself to the battle? So likewise ye, except ye utter by the tongue words easy to be understood, how shall it be known what is spoken? for ye shall speak into the air" (14:7-9). From the realm even of lifeless things illustrations can be drawn. Unless there is a proper interval between the sounds so that the ear can detect the melody, even the most beautiful musical instrument will produce but a meaningless noise. If the trumpet, used to summon soldiers to battle, does not give a clear call but instead an uncertain one, then the warriors will not grasp the intended order but will be left in confusion. Even so with that which is spoken to human beings—the words given out must be "easy to be understood," otherwise they are no more than empty sounds sent forth aimlessly into the air.

"There are, it may be, so many kinds of voices in the world, and none of them is without signification. Therefore if I know not the meaning of the voice, I shall be unto him that speaketh a barbarian, and he that speaketh shall be a barbarian unto me. Even so ye, forasmuch as ye are zealous of spiritual gifts, seek that ye may excel to the edifying of the church" (14:10-12). There are many languages in the world, says the apostle. (Some authorities now conclude that there are more than 3,000 languages on this earth!) Although each language has meaning to those who speak it, it is valueless to one who does not understand. Christians should seek to excel not in gifts that are valueless to others but in those that will edify the Body of Christ.

"Wherefore let him that speaketh in an unknown tongue pray that he may interpret. For if I pray in an unknown tongue, my spirit prayeth, but my understanding is unfruitful. What is it then? I will pray with the spirit, and I will pray with the understanding also: I will sing with the spirit, and I will sing with the understanding also. Else when thou shalt bless with the spirit, how shall he that occupieth the room of the unlearned say Amen at thy giving of thanks, seeing he understandeth not what thou sayest? For thou verily givest thanks well, but the other is not edified" (14:13-17). The apostle urges the one who speaks in a tongue to pray that he may be able to interpret that which he says. If one prays in a tongue he cannot understand, he may enjoy the emotional experience, even though failing to get real benefit from it through lack of understanding. For the sake of others as well as for himself, Paul desires to pray or sing in such a way as to be understood by one who "occupies the place of a private person" (literal rendering). He means one who has no gift of tongues and cannot understand what is said by the one who has. If such a person cannot grasp that which has been spoken, how can he say "Amen" and make the prayer truly his own?

"I thank my God, I speak with tongues more than ye all: yet in the church I had rather speak five words with my understanding, that by my voice I might teach others also, than ten thousand words in an unknown tongue" (14:18, 19). "It is interesting that Paul said he spoke with tongues more than any of them, and if he spoke with tongues he did so when he was alone, unless some other was there who could interpret. But even if he could speak with tongues, there was no value in it in the gathering of other men and women" (Morgan). The apostle forcefully affirms that in the church it is better to speak five clear words that can be comprehended by the hearers than 10,000 in a language no one understands.

"Brethren, be not children in understanding: howbeit in malice be ye children, but in understanding be men. In the law it is written, With men of other tongues and other lips will I speak unto this people; and yet for all that will they not hear me, saith the Lord. Wherefore tongues are for a sign, not to them that believe, but to them that believe not: but prophesying serveth not for them that believe not, but for them which believe" (14:20-22). It is evident that in a childish way the Corinthians were quite delighted with their gift of tongues. The apostle urges them to be, so far as evil things are concerned, like children, but with regard to discerning the better things to be like men, in other words, mature and thoughtful. Quoting Deuteronomy 28:49 and Isaiah 28:11, 12 he refers to the fact that Jehovah sent the strange tongue of the Assyrian conquerors as a judgment on the unbelieving Jews of the Old Testament period. Therefore tongues, he concludes, are not a sign to convert men, but rather to condemn those hardened in unbelief. In this connection Acts 2:13 should be carefully noted. On the other hand, *prophesying*—the plain preaching of God's Word—leads men to faith in Christ, and then onward in the Christian life. This is far better.

"If therefore the whole church be come together into one place, and all speak with tongues, and there come in those that are unlearned, or unbelievers, will they not say that ye are mad? But if all prophesy, and there come in one that believeth not, or one unlearned, he is convinced

of all, he is judged of all: and thus are the secrets of his
heart made manifest; and so falling down on his face he
will worship God, and report that God is in you of a
truth" (14:23-25). To further illustrate his teaching, Paul
imagines the whole church speaking in tongues. In comes
an unbeliever or a newly interested person seeking instruction. Instead of being blessed, such would consider
the Christians to be mad. On the other hand if all
prophesied, such people would be convicted by the Word
of God and would conclude that truly God was present
in that assembly.

"How is it then, brethren? when ye come together,
every one of you hath a psalm, hath a doctrine, hath a
tongue, hath a revelation, hath an interpretation. Let all
things be done unto edifying. If any man speak in an unknown tongue, let it be by two, or at the most three, and
that by course; and let one interpret. But if there be no
interpreter, let him keep silence in the church; and let
him speak to himself, and to God. Let the prophets
speak two or three, and let the other judge. If anything
be revealed to another that sitteth by, let the first hold his
peace. For ye may all prophesy one by one, that all may
learn, and all may be comforted. And the spirits of the
prophets are subject to the prophets. For God is not the
author of confusion, but of peace, as in all the churches
of the saints" (14:26-33). The apostle now gives definite
rules for the use of the gifts of tongues and of prophesying. The first precept is that all things be done "unto edifying." Tongues shall be spoken by not more than three,
and those shall speak not all at once but "by course."
Furthermore, if there be none able to interpret the
language, then those with the gift of tongues are to keep
silence altogether, speaking only inwardly to themselves

and to God. Those who prophesy are likewise to speak in order and only about three should speak at a single meeting. None is to create confusion on the claim that he cannot help himself, for "the spirits of the prophets are subject to the prophets." Any procedure which is confused or disorderly bears on its very face the evidence that it is *not* of God, "for God is not the author of confusion, but of peace."

"Let your women keep silence in the churches; for it is not permitted unto them to speak; but they are commanded to be under obedience, as also saith the law. And if they will learn anything, let them ask their husbands at home: for it is a shame for women to speak in the church. What? came the word of God out from you? or came it unto you only?" (14:34-36). These verses have, sad to say, been greatly twisted by well-meaning Christians. As already seen in chapter 7, unruly and self-assertive women were causing trouble in the Corinthian assembly. The present reference is to wives not chattering in church but rather speaking quietly with their husbands at a later time, if they have any real question. "Evidently there were women in Corinth given to careless and contentious talk, and that is what Paul was prohibiting. Certainly he was not saying that a woman had no right to pray or prophesy in the Church, because he had already given instructions as to how, and under what conditions, she was to do it. No, something else had crept into that fellowship meeting, the attitude taken by the women who were indulging in contentious, strident speech. Such were to keep silence there, and to remit the questions and discussions to the quietness and fellowship of the home" (Morgan). The Corinthians seemed to think they were the originators of the Word of God. They are reminded such is not the case—they were merely receivers of it.

"If any man think himself to be a prophet, or spiritual, let him acknowledge that the things that I write unto you are the commandments of the Lord. But if any man be ignorant, let him be ignorant" (14:37, 38). Paul makes the definite claim that the things he writes are "the commandments of the Lord." If anyone is really a spiritual person, or a prophet, he will acknowledge such to be the case. But if anyone chooses to remain willfully ignorant, then let him continue in his condition and bear the responsibility of it.

"Wherefore, brethren, covet to prophesy, and forbid not to speak with tongues. Let all things be done decently and in order" (14:39, 40). The apostle closes the discussion of this subject by once more emphasizing the desirability of the gift of prophecy. If any person truly has the gift of tongues, however, he should not be rejected so long as he abides by the proper rules which have been laid down. In everything the standard is this: "Let all things be done decently and in order." The Greek word here translated *decently* means *gracefully* or *becomingly*. So in the worship of the church everything is to be done gracefully and in an orderly manner.

Chapter Eight

ERRORS CORRECTED:
CONCERNING THE GOSPEL
(15:1-58)

THE INSTRUCTION GIVEN in this chapter was evidently for the purpose of meeting the situation mentioned in verse 12: "Now if Christ be preached that he rose from the dead, how say some among you that there is no resurrection of the dead?" Paul now shows that the full Gospel includes both the atoning death and resurrection of Jesus Christ, with His resurrection being the assurance of that of the believer. This is truly the great *resurrection* chapter of the entire Bible.

The first eleven verses present the Gospel message and the evidence for its truthfulness. "Moreover, brethren, I declare unto you the gospel which I preached unto you, which also ye have received, and wherein ye stand; by which also ye are saved, if ye keep in memory what I have preached unto you, unless ye have believed in vain" (15:1, 2). The Gospel Paul now declares was exactly the same which he had already preached to these people. By it they had been saved. "If ye keep in memory" is, in the original language, the grammatical form which assumes the thing stated to be true. It could be translated *"since* ye keep in memory." The matter of their believing "in vain" is explained more fully in verse 17: "And if Christ be not raised, your faith is vain; ye are yet in your sins."

"For I delivered unto you first of all that which I also received, how that Christ died for our sins according to the scriptures; and that he was buried, and that he rose again the third day according to the scriptures" (15:3, 4). The apostle had already delivered to them the Gospel he himself received from Christ. The essence of this Gospel is in the *atoning death* of Christ, the *burial* of Christ (this lays emphasis on the empty tomb which proves that His was not just a "spiritual resurrection"), and the glorious resurrection of Christ. His death and resurrection are said to be "according to the scriptures," which means that they accord with the Old Testament prophetic Scriptures.

"And that he was seen of Cephas, then of the twelve: after that, he was seen of above five hundred brethren at once; of whom the greater part remain unto this present, but some are fallen asleep. After that, he was seen of James; then of all the apostles. And last of all he was seen of me also, as of one born out of due time. For I am the least of the apostles, that am not meet to be called an apostle, because I persecuted the church of God. But by the grace of God I am what I am: and his grace which was bestowed upon me was not in vain; but I labored more abundantly than they all; yet not I, but the grace of God which was with me. Therefore whether it were I or they, so we preach, and so ye believed" (15:5-11). Testimony is now offered to establish the fact that Christ did rise in the body. This is both the great proof that the Gospel is true, and also the guarantee of our own bodily resurrection some day. The list of names given who observed the risen Lord is not exhaustive but representative: Peter, James, the apostles, the five hundred (doubtless the same referred to in Matt. 28:16-20), last of all Paul himself.

The Greek word Paul uses in describing himself as one "born out of due time" is that from which we get our English *abortion* (by transliteration). "Paul speaks of himself as having seen the risen Lord, and as one born out of due time. We are apt to think that this means that he was born much later than others, but the word he uses precludes any such thought. It really means, one born *before* the time. He is thinking of that glorious day when the risen, glorified Christ is to appear on earth once more, and His people Israel will look upon Him whom they have pierced, and as they recognize Him as their Lord and Saviour the nation will be born in a day. Paul had known that experience already. He first saw Christ in resurrection and, receiving Him as Saviour, became one of the new creation number" (Ironside). Because of his record as a persecutor, Paul feels that he is hardly fit to be called an apostle, but in all humility he recognizes that he has labored more than any of the rest, though all by the grace of God. He strongly affirms that both he and the rest of the apostles all preach the same identical Gospel.

Verses 12-19 reveal the essential nature of the resurrection of Christ so far as Christian truth is concerned. "Now if Christ be preached that he rose from the dead, how say some among you that there is no resurrection of the dead?" (15:12). It is clear that some of the Corinthians were affirming that there was no bodily resurrection, perhaps applying previous teaching Paul had given them on this subject to the new birth, which is a "spiritual resurrection" so to speak. While there is now no further information available to us as to the exact false teaching Paul was combating, it is well known that the ancient Greeks believed in the immortality of the soul but not in bodily resurrection.

"But if there be no resurrection of the dead, then is Christ not risen: and if Christ be not risen, then is our preaching vain, and your faith is also vain. Yea, and we are found false witnesses of God; because we have testified of God that he raised up Christ: whom he raised not up, if so be that the dead rise not. For if the dead rise not, then is not Christ raised: and if Christ be not raised, your faith is vain; ye are yet in your sins. Then they also which are fallen asleep in Christ are perished. If in this life only we have hope in Christ, we are of all men most miserable" (15:13-19). These heretical teachers, though not directly denying the resurrection of Christ, were nevertheless unwittingly rejecting it. Since Christ became a true Man, if the dead rise not, says Paul, "then is not Christ risen." It must be emphasized that the argument which follows in the rest of the chapter has nothing whatsoever to do with the fact that the *soul* of a believer lives on after death. This all admitted. The apostle's teaching relates specifically to the resurrection of the *body.* If Christ did not rise in the body, then all the apostolic preaching is vain and empty. The faith of Christians is also vain. If Christ did not rise, then the apostles are liars, and believers are reposing their hope in a vain pretense, being actually still lost sinners. Dead Christians have perished forever, going to a lost eternity instead of a blessed paradise. Living Christians are miserable men who have sacrificed the selfish pleasures of this present world for that which is a deceitful mirage. All this—"if Christ be not risen."

But Christ *did* rise, and His resurrection is the guarantee of the resurrection of believers as well as of the final triumph of His kingdom. "But now is Christ risen from the dead, and become the first fruits of them that slept. For since by man came death, by man came also the resurrection of the dead. For as in Adam all die, even so in Christ shall all be made alive" (15:20-22). "But now" —blessed words! All the foregoing was untrue—Christ *did* rise from the dead, and our faith is *not* in vain. The Lord Jesus is the *first fruits*. The allusion is to Leviticus 23:11. On the day following the Passover Sabbath, the first sheaf of the new crop was presented in the temple, with a sacrifice. This acknowledged that all came from God, and none should be used until this part had been returned to Him. It was also a sample, or specimen, of the bounteous harvest soon to come through His loving provision. The Lord Jesus is in His resurrection *the* first fruits. By man—Adam—came death. By another Man— Christ—comes the resurrection of the dead. All related to Adam die. This includes the whole human race (Gen. 3:19; Rom. 5:12). The statement that "in Christ all shall be made alive" again refers to the whole human race, not just the saved. Christ's mighty power will some day call forth all from the grave. Their relation to Him will determine their future destiny.

"But every man in his own order: Christ the first fruits; afterward they that are Christ's at his coming. Then cometh the end, when he shall have delivered up the kingdom to God, even the Father; when he shall have put down all rule and all authority and power. For he must reign, till he hath put all enemies under his feet. The last enemy that shall be destroyed is death" (15:23-26). All people will not however be raised from the dead at the same time, but "each in his own order." The Greek word here translated *order* is "especially a military term, denoting a company" (Vine). Revelation 20 makes it clear that the dead are raised in two groups with the Millennium coming between. The total resurrection is said then to be in three "companies," so to speak: (1) "Christ, the first fruits," some 1900 years ago; (2) "they that are Christ's at his coming," whenever that may be; (3) and finally "the end" resurrection, at the close of the millennial period. Then at that time the Lord Jesus will have finally and completely put down all hostile power and authority. Even death itself will at last be destroyed. Death is "destroyed" in the sense that all its victims are taken from it and never again will there be such a thing.

"For he hath put all things under his feet. But when he saith, all things are put under him, it is manifest that he is excepted, which did put all things under him. And when all things shall be subdued unto him, then shall the Son also himself be subject unto him that put all things under him, that God may be all in all" (15:27, 28). Verse 27 is an allusion to Psalm 8:6, and the pronouns must be carefully distinguished if the meaning is to be clear. The apostle is saying that the Father has put all things under the Son's feet. But when the Father says this about the Son it is manifest that the statement does not include the Father Himself who put all things under the Son's feet. Everything else is to be subject to the Son, the Son Himself will be subject to the Father, and God will be "all in all." In other words the day will finally have come when each being shall say: "God is everything to me." It should be carefully noted that "the deliverance of the kingdom unto God, and the subjection of the Son to the

Father, do not mean that Christ is to cease to reign, or that He is not divine" (Erdman).

An important but sometimes neglected fact is by these verses made clear: the millennial reign is *not* the final stage of Christ's kingdom. During the Millennium, wonderful as it will be, there are still hostile powers waiting their opportunity to rise up against the Lord Jesus. After all these are put under foot, the kingdom enters a new stage, but Christ Himself reigns on throughout eternity.

"Else what shall they do which are baptized for the dead, if the dead rise not at all? why are they then baptized for the dead? And why stand we in jeopardy every hour? I protest by your rejoicing which I have in Christ Jesus our Lord, I die daily. If after the manner of men I have fought with beasts at Ephesus, what advantageth it me, if the dead rise not? let us eat and drink; for to-morrow we die. Be not deceived: evil communications corrupt good manners. Awake to righteousness, and sin not; for some have not the knowledge of God: I speak this to your shame" (15:29-34). In this passage Paul asserts that if the great facts previously stated were not true, then it would be useless to live as a Christian now. If the resurrection were not a reality, then it would be useless to be "baptized for the dead." Exactly what Paul means by this latter expression seems impossible to say. Reliable commentators differ widely in their views. To be rejected is the idea that this means a living person could be baptized for a dead *unsaved* friend, for this would contradict the general teaching of Scripture. Also to be refused is the suggestion that Christians of that day were baptized for *saved* friends who had died without baptism. There is no record whatsoever of such a practice in the early Church.

Two interpretations have been offered either of which seems reasonable and scripturally acceptable. (1) The reference here is to those "who, through the introductory rite of baptism, are taking the places in the ranks left vacant by Christians who have died" (Scofield). (2) The expression refers to non-Christians, who after the death of Christian loved ones sought the Lord and were baptized so that they might some day see those saved loved ones again, is believed by Dr. Erdman to be the thought here.

Furthermore, says the apostle, sacrifice in Christian service such as he was making would be useless if there was no resurrection. In such a case the common saying of godless people would be true: "Let us eat and drink; for tomorrow we die." The allusion to fighting with beasts at Ephesus, if taken literally, is the only reference in the entire New Testament to such an event in the life of Paul. Most Bible expositors think he is referring to his experiences there with "beastly men," for example in the riot of the idolatrous silversmiths against him.

The apostle closes the paragraph with a reference to the fact that some of the Corinthians were being deceived through listening to the ideas of ungodly people. He calls on them to awake as from a drunken stupor (for that is the import of the Greek), and to listen no more to those who willfully know not God. To heed such is shameful.

"But some man will say, How are the dead raised up? and with what body do they come? Thou fool, that which thou sowest is not quickened, except it die: and that which thou sowest, thou sowest not that body that shall be, but bare grain, it may chance of wheat, or of some other grain: but God giveth it a body as it hath pleased him, and to every seed his own body. All flesh is not the same flesh: but there is one kind of flesh of men, another flesh of beasts, another of fishes, and another of birds. There are also celestial bodies, and bodies terrestrial: but the glory of the celestial is one, and the glory of the terrestrial is another. There is one glory of the sun, and another glory of the moon, and another glory of the stars: for one star differeth from another star in glory" (15:35-41). The apostle now turns to the *nature of the resurrection body*. This discussion he opens by quoting two questions which foolish objectors raise: "How are the dead raised up?" "With what body do they come?" "The first question implies that resurrection is impossible; the second, that it is inconceivable" (Erdman).

Paul answers by an analogy from nature. A seed is buried in the earth. To all appearances it dies. Later it rises to a larger and more glorious life. This illustration is not intended to prove the *fact* of the resurrection. That has already been done. The picture rather reveals something of the *nature* of the resurrection body. It will be the same body, and yet different too. This should not seem strange for there are different kinds of bodies here on earth in the animal kingdom. There are also differences in bodies adapted to the heavenly realm and those adapted to the earthly realm. There are even distinctions between the heavenly orbs—sun, moon, and stars. Among the stars "one star differeth from another star in glory." "Like flowers the stars have their own colors. At your first upward glance all gleam white as frost crystals, but single out this one and that for observation and you will find a subtle spectrum in the stars. The quality of their lights is determined by their temperatures. . . . In the December sky you will see Aldebaran as pale rose, Regel, bluish white; Betelgeuse orange to topaz yellow" (Donald Peattie in the *Reader's Digest*).

"So also is the resurrection of the dead. It is sown in corruption; it is raised in incorruption: it is sown in dishonor; it is raised in glory: it is sown in weakness; it is raised in power: it is sown a natural body; it is raised a spiritual body. There is a natural body, and there is a spiritual body. And so it is written, The first man Adam was made a living soul; the last Adam was made a quickening spirit. Howbeit that was not first which is spiritual, but that which is natural; and afterward that which is spiritual. The first man is of the earth, earthy: the second man is the Lord from heaven. As is the earthy, such are they also that are earthy: and as is the heavenly, such are they also that are heavenly. And as we have borne the image of the earthy, we shall also bear the image of the heavenly" (15:42-49). In the resurrection the present body will be changed. It is buried now as a corrupt, weak, natural body. In the resurrection it will become incorruptible, powerful, glorious, spiritual. The present body is a "natural body." It is adapted to the earthly realm. The resurrection body will be a "spiritual body." It will be adapted to the heavenly realm. The first Adam was made by God a "living soul." Christ, the "last Adam" is a "life-giving spirit." All of us originally belonged to the old race descended from Adam. From him we partook of that which was "earthy." Christ is also the head of a race—the New Creation. From Him we who are His shall some day bear "his image."

"Now this I say, brethren, that flesh and blood cannot inherit the kingdom of God; neither doth corruption inherit incorruption. Behold I show you a mystery; We shall not all sleep, but we shall all be changed, in a moment, in the twinkling of an eye, at the last trump: for the trumpet shall sound, and the dead shall be raised incorruptible, and we shall be changed. For this corruptible must put on incorruption, and this mortal must put on immortality. So when this corruptible shall have put on incorruption, and this mortal shall have put on immortality, then shall be brought to pass the saying that is written, Death is swallowed up in victory. O death, where is thy sting? O grave, where is thy victory? The sting of death is sin; and the strength of sin is the law. But thanks be to God, which giveth us the victory through our Lord Jesus Christ. Therefore, my beloved brethren, be ye steadfast, unmovable, always abounding in the work of the Lord, forasmuch as ye know that your labor is not in vain in the Lord" (15:50-58). A *mystery* is now revealed: some believers will never die. All Christians will not pass through death (which Paul calls "sleep") but all will be changed from the earthly to the heavenly. This shall take place "in a moment" when the trumpet sounds for the Rapture (see I Thess. 4:16). Dead Christians will then be raised. Living Christians will be translated, as were Enoch and Elijah in the Old Testament. Verse 53 doubtless refers to the dead Christians as "corruptible" and to the living Christians as "mortal." These must "put on" respectively "incorruption" and "immortality." When this takes place then Isaiah 25:8 will be a reality: "Death is swallowed up in victory." In verse 55 "the apostle places himself and his readers in the presence of the Saviour and the risen dead and the transformed living arrayed in immortality, and in view of that majestic scene he breaks out in these words of triumph" (Hodge).

Sin caused death. Sin gave to death its fatal power. So

it is easy to see why Paul says that "the sting of death is sin." It is not so easy to understand what he means when he says "the strength of sin is the law." Perhaps the allusion is to the fact that though the law is holy and good, man being sinful in nature is unable to keep it, so to him it becomes a death sentence (see Rom. 7:9-14). But God gives us the victory through Christ even over death. In view of this certain triumph, Christians should even now be "always abounding in the work of the Lord."

Chapter Nine

ERRORS CORRECTED:
CONCERNING MONEY
(16:1-9)

NOW CONCERNING THE COLLECTION for the saints, as I have given order to the churches of Galatia, even so do ye" (16:1). A collection for the poor believers at Jerusalem seems to have been a project especially dear to the heart of Paul (cf. Rom. 15:26; Acts 24:17). This was no doubt true because of their great need there, and also because of a promise the apostle had made at the time of the Jerusalem Council (Gal. 2:10). In addition it would be an excellent means of drawing Jewish and Gentile believers into closer fellowship with one another. About this matter Paul now repeats instructions previously given in Galatia. "These instructions are of the very greatest value to the churches of today. Together with the other intimations of this paragraph, they embody most of the necessary principles of Christian beneficence and church finance" (Erdman).

"Upon the first day of the week let every one of you lay by him in store, as God hath prospered him, that there be no gatherings when I come. And when I come, whomsoever ye shall approve by your letters, them will I send to bring your liberality unto Jerusalem. And if it be meet that I go also, they shall go with me. Now I will come unto you, when I shall pass through Macedonia: for I do pass through Macedonia. And it may be that I will abide, yea, and winter with you, that ye may bring me on my journey whithersoever I go. For I will not see you now by the way; but I trust to tarry a while with you, if the Lord permit. But I will tarry at Ephesus until Pentecost. For a great door and effectual is opened unto me, and there are many adversaries" (16:2-9).

Let us take up these verses in which several important principles are enunciated: (1) Offerings are to be made regularly—"on the first day of the week." This, by the way, shows that the *first day* was already observed by Christians as the Lord's Day. (2) *Every* person was to have a part in the offering, whether rich or poor. (3) Each was however to give *proportionately*—"as God hath prospered him." (4) Giving is not to be merely in response to occasional special appeals—"no gatherings when I come." (5) Christian finances should be carefully handled by able representatives chosen by the people. (6) Christian offerings should be *liberal*.

Paul gives a personal word indicating that he plans to come to Corinth, but only after a length of time. He must first pass through Macedonia. So he intends to pay a longer visit later rather than a brief one now. Meantime he must stay at Ephesus for a while longer. There are great opportunities there for him to seize as well as "many adversaries" to combat.

Chapter Ten

CLOSING ADMONITIONS
(16:10-24)

Now if Timotheus come, see that he may be with you without fear: for he worketh the work of the Lord, as I also do. Let no man therefore despise him: but conduct him forth in peace, that he may come unto me: for I look for him with the brethren. As touching our brother Apollos, I greatly desired him to come unto you with the brethren: but his will was not at all to come at this time; but he will come when he shall have a convenient time" (16:10-12). Paul urges a cordial reception for Timothy, and indicates that Apollos will visit them later. It may be that the reason Apollos did not wish to see them just then was because of the present state of things in which they were setting off him against Paul and Peter.

"Watch ye, stand fast in the faith, quit you like men, be strong. Let all your things be done with love" (16:13, 14). These are general instructions for all. All are admonished to be watchful, steadfast, courageous, strong, loving.

"I beseech you, brethren (ye know the house of Stephanas, that it is the first fruits of Achaia, and that they have addicted themselves to the ministry of the saints,) that ye submit yourselves unto such, and to everyone that helpeth with us, and laboreth. I am glad of the coming of Stephanas and Fortunatus and Achaicus: for that which was lacking on your part they have supplied. For they have refreshed my spirit and yours: therefore acknowledge ye them that are such" (16:15-18). The apostle speaks of his pleasure over fellowship he has had with certain Corinthians. These are people who have "addicted themselves to the ministry of the saints." Such should be recognized.

"The churches of Asia salute you. Aquila and Priscilla salute you much in the Lord, with the church that is in their house. All the brethren greet you. Greet ye one another with an holy kiss" (16:19, 20). Aquila and Priscilla join in greetings to the Corinthians, as do all the believers at Ephesus, from which city Paul wrote.

"The salutation of me Paul with mine own hand. If any man love not the Lord Jesus Christ, let him be Anathema Maran-atha. The grace of our Lord Jesus Christ be with you. My love be with you all in Christ Jesus. Amen" (16:21-24). Paul usually wrote his letters through a "stenographer." It was his custom, however, to sign his name at the close. This he now does. He says that if anyone professes to be a follower of Christ but does not really love Him, "let him be accursed" (the meaning of Anathema). *Maran-atha* means "the Lord is coming." This may likely have been an expression used frequently among the early Christians as a kind of greeting. The apostle closes with his usual benediction centering around the *grace* of the Lord Jesus Christ. Since he had to administer some unpleasant rebukes in the letter it is quite fitting that his very last word is a strong expression of his love for the Corinthians.